THE
THREE DAYS

PARISH PRAYER IN THE PASCHAL TRIDUUM

THE THREE DAYS

PARISH PRAYER IN THE PASCHAL TRIDUUM

GABE HUCK

LITURGY TRAINING PUBLICATIONS

Acknowledgments

This work is dedicated to Sister Polycarp and the community of Missionary Benedictine Sisters at whose convent in Norfolk, Nebraska, the Vigil was celebrated with great beauty and joy in the early 1950s; to the monks of Conception Abbey in Missouri who kept the Vigil in 1956 in a manner I shall never forget; to all those who, since the first publication of this book, have talked to me about the Triduum and have helped me see these life-giving days more clearly. I am grateful to several people in particular: to the authors of the *Sourcebook for Sundays and Seasons* over the years, Peter Scagnelli, Peter Mazar and Thomas Ryan; to Kathy Luty; to Brian Helge (may he rest in peace); to Diana Kodner Sotak and Ken Sotak with whom I have done many workshops on this subject; to all those, named and unnamed, whose insights I have borrowed for these pages.

The woodcuts on the cover and throughout the book are the work of Santa Barbara artist Nina Morlan. The design of the book is by Jill Smith. Elizabeth Hoffman and Peter Mazar, editors at LTP, read and made suggestions on the manuscript. Copyediting was done by Theresa Pincich and typesetting by James Mellody-Pizzato. The text is set in Univers Extra Bold and Sabon. The Three Days has been printed and bound by Northwestern Printing House of Chicago.

Liturgy Training Publications, 1800 North Hermitage Avenue, Chicago IL 60622-1101; 1-800-933-1800; FAX 1-800-933-7094.

Printed in the United States of America

ISBN 0-929650-51-4
3D/R

          Library of Congress Cataloging-in-Publication Data
Huck, Gabe.
     The three days: parish prayer in the Paschal Triduum/Gabe Huck.
   —Rev. ed.
       p. cm.
    ISBN 0-929650-51-4: $11.95
    1. Paschal Triduum—Liturgy. 2. Catholic Church—Liturgy.
  I. Title.
  BX2015.785.H83 1992   91-43792
  264'.02—dc20   CIP

CONTENTS

Foreword to the Revised Edition

Fourteen years ago, I prepared several pamphlets on the liturgies of the Triduum. In 1981, these evolved into a book called *The Three Days*. Now we have had another decade to experience the Triduum and the impact of adult initiation in Catholic parishes. Much of what was said in the earlier edition can stand, but it has seemed better to rework the whole text. The basic format of the previous edition was helpful to those using the book and has been retained.

The initial chapter is both universal and particular. It attempts to present the centrality of the Triduum in the life of a church, then goes on to deal with the seemingly small matters of rehearsals and schedules. What joins universals and particulars is this: Without a grasp of the former and a commitment to the latter, the best efforts for good and consistent parish practice in liturgy will not come to much.

After this essential introduction, the chapters follow the Triduum from evening on Holy Thursday until the Vespers of Easter Sunday afternoon. Much of this material deals with the principal rites of the Three Days: the place of each liturgy in the time itself, an understanding of the movement within each rite, and a detailed examination of everything that is peculiar to these assemblies.

This volume includes additional material in the appendix, where various sections deal with different approaches to catechesis on the Triduum, with the making of the Easter candle and baptismal garments, and with other practical matters.

What is missing? There is no attention to ethnic traditions that in some places should be an important part of keeping the Triduum. Little is said here of the history of these rites and the seasons that surround them. Some references will be found in the bibliography (see appendix, part 4). The role of music and the task of music at specific points is discussed, but there is no effort to offer extensive lists of possible selections.

This book is intended for those persons who prepare the liturgies of the Triduum in parishes. Perhaps even more basically, it is addressed to those who have leadership roles in the parish even if not all of these persons take part in the preparation of the liturgy or assume a ministry at the liturgy.

These Days Embrace All

It is so addressed because we have to begin implementing what we believe: that the rites of the church—of the local church, the incarnation of church—express and shape the life of the church, the life of baptized people. Lent, Triduum and Eastertime—together the paschal season—are the clearest expression of this. We believe that if Lent is kept by a parish, it seeps into every part of that parish's life and into every part of every household that makes up that parish. We believe that the arrival of Triduum is then all absorbing. We also believe that Eastertime is a presence felt in all activities and missions of the parish. Here and there, little by little, are the signs that this can be so in this place and time. It takes years of steady effort. It takes paying attention to the world.

This is different from saying that during these seasons, Triduum especially, the "liturgists" emerge and have their say and the other staff members and committees fade to the background. Yes, the liturgies of these seasons and days require care, and that has to involve preparation, rehearsal, great attention. But these seasons are not their liturgies. *The days themselves, lived by catechumens and baptized Christians, are our Lent, our Triduum, our Eastertime.* The liturgies are nourishment and insight, and they are the constant reminders that we are in this as a church not as so many individuals. That is what the liturgies are, things unintelligible apart from baptized people living their Lent, Triduum, Easter.

Every Christian—certainly everyone with a leadership role in the community—needs to understand something of how the keeping of these seasons molds the community in its discipline and tradition. We need to know, in other words, that the keeping of such days through our years is what makes a Christian. Even more, they make the church.

Much of this text may dwell on the order of a service or on the excellence needed in some ministry. Such things are important, for the principal rites lay a foundation for the lives Christians live. But everyone need not be concerned with such attention to details. What has to concern the leadership (besides making sure that there are qualified persons to attend to such details) is all the ways that Lent, Triduum and Eastertime become nothing less than the way of life for this Catholic community. That intention is deep in every page of this book. As a matter of simple order, such a direction ought to surface yearly in staff, parish council and other forums that guide parish life.

The significance of these days and the seasons that surround them should be a matter of discussion at parish staff and even parish council meetings. Such discussion happens because, gradually, for these leaders there is a sense of how their own lives and their communal life are bound to the keeping of these days. That is the source of their zeal that this be so for the whole parish. (At some point, the pamphlet "Introduction to Lent and Eastertime" [LTP] might serve as background reading and a springboard for discussion in staff or council meetings.)

What is so difficult in this time and place is recovering a sense that a people (a church) can and must set days aside and then so keep such days that the days and their observance will re-create the people (the church). Such a way of being in time is hard for us. We want time to be ours, to be shaped to our various economic and private needs and schedules. But as the church we try to grasp that time is not ours but God's. We try to see that the lifelong work of becoming the church means a discipline that is written down in time itself, in the simple truth that a day comes called Ash Wednesday and—no other options—the church enters and keeps Lent. Forty hard but lifegiving days later we stand at the brink of the Triduum.

That it is Lent, Triduum, Eastertime is somehow to be pervasive, to penetrate every move we make, every breath we draw, in those days. That probably cannot be until and unless we take into ourselves what was contained in a single, wonderful Latin word, *hodie.* Today. "This is the night," the Exsultet sings. Today. Tonight. *This* time. When that is forgotten, we can marry and take holidays during Lent, we can nibble through the Triduum, we can believe that an inspiring Holy Thursday liturgy met the only criterion. For now, we have to search for whatever it will take to get *hodie* back into ourselves and our church. The Vigil is our best hope of this. *All* of time, every *hodie,* is drawn into this night. We have to demand and expect this.

About the Vocabulary

Because there are numerous references to the rites of initiation in these pages, the vocabulary is that of the order of Christian initiation of adults. "Catechumens" are those who have been received into the order of catechumens but have not yet been called, in the rite of election, to prepare for the Easter sacraments. As parishes become comfortable with the need for some persons to remain in the catechumenate a year or longer, it will be common to have catechumens present during Lent who are not "elect." The "elect" are, strictly speaking, catechumens also, but "elect" will be used here for those catechumens who have been chosen (elected) at the beginning of Lent to be baptized and confirmed at the Easter Vigil, then to join the church at the eucharistic table. Catechumens, then, are called the "elect" only for one Lent and the first two days of the Triduum. "Neophytes" is used interchangeably with "newly baptized." "Candidates" will refer to those who, already baptized, have prepared for reception into full communion with the Catholic church.

Another term that may cause confusion is "vigil." Vigil is our only way to designate the entire rite of the night between Saturday and Sunday. If it is not yet understood by some Catholics as being the preeminent liturgy of Easter (and therefore including the eucharistic liturgy), that is a problem of catechesis, not vocabulary. This liturgy has a name and does not need another. In this volume, the notion of "vigiling" also is used occasionally to mean the stance of the whole church during the two days that climax in the Vigil liturgy of Saturday night. To speak of "keeping watch" or "keeping vigil" during Friday and Saturday seems entirely appropriate. We need this term or some single verb that says *what we do* during the whole of the time between Thursday night and Saturday night. When we can't name what we're doing, we're likely not to know that these days are different.

Finally, there is the word "triduum" itself. Many people have trouble pronouncing it even after they know what it means. It is a Latin word meaning "three days" and has been used for other three-day periods but now seems reserved to the Easter or the Paschal Triduum. The alternative to Triduum might be simply "Easter," or a word truer to the roots, "Passover" or "Pasch." But these words already have other primary meanings. Would we be better off using (as the title of this book does) "the Three Days" or "the Easter Three Days" to render this strange word "triduum" in English? They are long and they may not sound enough like a name, but they can well serve as alternatives. Perhaps then it is worth the trouble of learning the new word "triduum" (and learning to pronounce it), for it denotes a reality we did not have with us before the revision of the calendar. In parishes where the keeping of Lent and the rituals of the initiation of adults and the centrality of these three days have emerged over the past 20 years, ordinary Catholics now speak of the Triduum as something they know well.

People will continue to speak of "Holy Week." Perhaps in calendars and bulletins we should avoid that term, focusing instead on the final days of Lent that pass quietly into the Triduum. But "Holy Week" was a useful term and it did its job. Perhaps one day "Triduum" will be that clearly defined and universally recognized in the church.

One further clarification relates to the 1988 *Circular Letter* sent by the Vatican's Congregation for Divine Worship to the conferences of bishops. This document does not itself break new ground, but organizes many earlier notes and responses into a useful format. It is available from the Publishing Services of the U.S. Catholic Conference as *Circular Letter Concerning the Preparation and Celebration of the Easter Triduum*. In this book it is usually referred to as the *Circular Letter*.

The dialogue involved in the evolution of this book will continue. During the past few years, the notes appearing in the annual *Sourcebook for Sundays and Seasons* (LTP) have kept this dialogue moving, and they have been much used in these pages. Those who read this book are invited to communicate further ideas and/or criticisms on individual points or on the approach taken here. I would welcome your reactions and suggestions.

Gabe Huck

The Triduum

For Christians, our every year has its origin and its climax at a time determined by the earth and the sun and the moon and the human-made cycle of a seven-day week. The marvelous accidents of earth's place and sun's place, of axis and of orbit make cycles within human cycles so that days can be named and remembered and rhythms established.

First, we wait for the angle of the earth's axis to make day and night equal (going toward longer days in the "top" half of earth, longer nights in the other half). Then we wait for the moon to be full. Then we wait for the Lord's Day and call that particular Lord's Day "Easter" in English, but in most other Western languages some word that is closer to an old name, "Pesach" or "Pascha," made into English as "Passover."

In these generations, we are finding out how, on the night between Saturday and that Sunday, the church ends and begins not just its year but its very self.

We do not come to this night unaware. The church has spent the time since Thursday evening in intense preparation. Even more, we have had the 40 days of Lent to tear down and to build up toward this night.

And the night needs a week of weeks, 50 days, afterward to unfold. The 50 days are Eastertime; only after Pentecost does life return to normal.

The church came very early to keep something of the spring festival known to Jesus and the first followers. They were Jews and that first full moon of spring was Passover. For those who followed Jesus, whether Jew or Gentile, this was the time when the story of the deliverance they proclaimed in the death and resurrection of Christ was placed beside the story already told at this festival, the deliverance of the captive people from the Pharaoh. Very early, that proclamation came to be made not in words alone but in the waters where those who were ready to stake everything on such a deliverance, on this Christ and this church, passed over in God's saving deed.

In our time, following the Second Vatican Council, Roman Catholics and some other Christian churches have reclaimed their tradition. We have begun to experience how the rhythm of the year is, in large part, the rhythm of initiation. Once a year seems the right rhythm for summoning the elect to the font. Once a year is as often as we can put ourselves through this night, for it takes those many days to approach it and another many days to get over it. We have named a day in the year's cycle when we walk to the waters. We work ourselves up to drawing other persons into those waters. Doing that, we have all we can take of baptism for a long time. We cannot have catechumens prepared more often than this. We cannot be this serious and this beautiful and this painfully close to the waters more than once a year.

In the years since Vatican II, we have begun to discover how this can be. That will take a generation yet, for it is never a matter of simply imitating ancient ways (though from those ways we can learn much: See the account of initiation in the early church in the appendix, part 1). We have to be the church in the midst of our own times. But fundamental directions have been taken. In 1969, the Council's teaching on the shape of the liturgical year was spelled out in *General Norms for the Liturgical Year and the Calendar*. That document talks about the cycle of the year and names the principal elements. It begins not with Advent or with Lent but with this center of time for us:

> *Easter Triduum*. Christ redeemed us all and gave perfect glory to God principally through his paschal mystery: Dying he destroyed our death and rising he restored our life. Therefore the Easter Triduum of the passion and resurrection of Christ is the culmination of the entire liturgical year. Thus the solemnity of Easter has the same kind of preeminence in the liturgical year that Sunday has in the week.

> The Easter Triduum begins with the evening Mass of the Lord's Supper,
> reaches its high point in the Easter Vigil, and closes with evening prayer
> on Easter Sunday.

For the past several centuries, Lent had been counted up to Holy
Saturday noon. The Easter Vigil itself had come to be celebrated on
Saturday morning (in nearly empty churches) until the 1950s. Most
Catholics thought of Easter as the anniversary of Christ's resurrection, or simply as the end of Lent.

A few years after this revision of the calendar came the Rite of
Christian Initiation of Adults (RCIA). Here was a revolution: Conversion is to be manifest and supported in public, in the assembly,
and this is to happen within the rhythms of the church's seasons.
Initiation into this church is the constant and visible work of the
whole church, central and vital: When we initiate others, we
confront and renew our own identity.

The RCIA offers a pattern by which the adult who seeks to know
more about the Christ and the church may, after a time of inquiry,
ask to enter the catechumenate. Catechumens then spend months or
years experiencing the teachings and the ways of the church within a
parish community. At the beginning of Lent each year, that church
calls to the sacraments of initiation those catechumens who are
judged ready. These are the elect, the chosen. During Lent, they and
all the church with them prepare: Fasting, prayer and giving alms
now are as ever the disciplines of this Lent. On three lenten Sundays,
the church publicly prays over the elect; these scrutinies ritualize
what is happening in the struggle to reject evil and choose Christ.
The elect publicly receive the creed and the Lord's Prayer during
Lent and are told to learn them by heart.

All of this is not an added attraction during the parish Lent. It *is*
Lent. The *General Norms for the Liturgical Year and the Calendar*
describe the season:

> Lent is a preparation for the celebration of Easter. For the lenten liturgy
> disposes both catechumens and the faithful to celebrate the paschal
> mystery: catechumens, through the several stages of Christian initiation;
> the faithful, through reminders of their own baptism and through
> penitential practices.

Lent, for the elect and the baptized, has an intensity that we could not sustain year-round. Nonessential activities cease and essential activities are permeated with the ashes, exorcisms, psalms, prayers, fasting, almsgiving, scriptures, meditation and struggles that fill the local church's 40 days. This is our yearly approach to that "paschal mystery," a term best defined by the acclamations we know from the eucharistic prayer: "Dying you destroyed our death, rising you restored our life. Lord Jesus, come in glory."

Paschal mystery: Christ, the church, ourselves are "paschal," are "passover," are wound and bound together, battling to the death with death in all its faces, evil in all its faces. Precisely in the daily life of ordinary people is this passover, this passage of God and of ourselves realized. Lent means clarity, stripping down and stripping away so that we can see, taste, smell and touch the world because all of this is only for the life of the world. Such a Lent demands a serious sense of purpose and cheerful example by parish leadership, as it demands a continuity year to year so that its keeping becomes a virtue, a habit.

Toward evening on Holy Thursday, Lent ends. The church enters the Paschal or Easter Triduum. During Friday and Saturday, the elect and the whole church are called to fast and to pray. This fasting is not the lenten fast of discipline and of repentance. It is the excited, nervous fasting of anticipation. Our staying away from food (and much else) is like the disappearance of hunger in a bride and a groom before their wedding, in lovers long separated before their reunion. It is fasting from food and drink but also from work and entertainment and the myriad distractions.

Periodically, the church gathers to pray during these days, slowly building toward the prolonged vigiling of Saturday night. That Vigil in the darkness becomes an awesome and lengthy recital of our foundation, our scriptures. Then, when the great communion of saints has been invoked and the Spirit called on to enter these waters, when the elect have firmly renounced evil, these elect profess their faith in the Father, Son and Holy Spirit, and so the church baptizes and confirms and gathers these now wet and sweet-smelling people at table for eucharist. It makes for an amazing, hard, wonderful night. Sunday morning and afternoon blend into the first day of the Fifty Days, Eastertime, when we all learn to live with what has happened this night.

The only real preparation for Triduum is Lent and the journey with the elect. The only effective preparation for one Lent and Triduum and Eastertime is the Lent, Triduum and Eastertime of the year before and of the year before that and on and on.

Preparing the Parish

But when the importance of these days is becoming more clear, when efforts like those described in this book are being made so that indeed we have prepared well for the people to come and celebrate their liturgies, then are there ways to talk with the parish about the liturgies of the Triduum?

The preaching of Lent, the presence of the elect at the Sunday liturgies and their week-after-week dismissal before the intercessions, communal "fasting meals" and lenten charity and scripture study and prayer—all of these lean eagerly toward Easter. Sometimes that has to be explicit. It can be said that we will bring the money gathered by fasting (in the "Rice Bowls" of Catholic Relief Services, for example) to the liturgy of Holy Thursday evening where it will be gathered in that day's collection. It can be said in the dismissal of the elect: We speak of our eagerness for the time when they will join us at the table. We need not overdo, but neither should we miss what is simply Lent itself.

There is a wonderful catechesis built into consistent thinking about the Triduum. For example, the invitation to keep the days and attend the liturgies should be action as well as words. Are drivers available to pick up those who cannot come without assistance? Is child care available during the liturgies, at the parish or even in the homes in the case of the Vigil?

More explicit catechesis, at least for several years, may be needed. Many people simply have never heard about the way the church tries to keep the Triduum. Many have only some notions of Thursday as the anniversary of the Last Supper and Friday of the Passion. Sometimes this turns into a "passion play" attitude toward the Triduum, expecting the liturgies to be historical reenactments. But the notion of anniversary itself is something to build on. An anniversary is a remembering, and remembering is the wellspring of all Christian liturgy, including the Triduum. Our "anniversaries" see the present in light of what founded us, saved us, constituted us as a church. These days are filled with such remembering: of Christ's passion and death and resurrection, of our own baptism into that mystery.

Homilies on the Fifth Sunday of Lent and on Passion Sunday could be honest lenten homilies and still be strong invitations to keep the Triduum, including participation in its liturgies. In fact, every true lenten homily by its nature will be a summons toward the Triduum. Whether this is done or not, the parish bulletin can do far more than announce the times of services. The bulletin, at least on Passion Sunday, could forgo its usual appearance and attend only to the urgent matter of announcing the Triduum as it is to be kept in homes and lives and in the church itself. (See the appendix, part 2, for an example of the bulletin material; see the appendix, part 3, for an example of a Palm Sunday homily.)

This will be discussed in the chapter entitled "The Paschal Fast"; it should be part of any discussion about catechesis. The point of the catechesis cannot be merely the promotion of attendance at the liturgies, worthy and necessary as that is. What all of us lack to one extent or another is an understanding that it is the keeping of these days themselves that we need. If in these three days we are invited "to go to church," it is because going to church is something people keeping these days will need and want to do. Of course, being at the liturgies is itself incentive and invitation to maintain a vigil and fast and pray and keep moving toward the Easter feast. Here are three days whose once-a-year presence is meant to be total in our lives. We want to convey this, but we have few analogies. Perhaps Thanksgiving and Christmas, for some, are such days, days whose presence permeates every moment so that even the little business-as-usual that gets done is transformed.

The direction then is toward what these days might look like in people's lives, what a gift they are meant to be, how they bring us together in our assembly at various times. Examples can be helpful to a point. It helps to know that a couple with three young children keeps the Triduum with simple meals, a special time of making very creative Easter eggs, a long time in a park. Or a single, professional person puts everything away that has to do with work, unplugs the television, fasts except for juice, reads the psalms and John's gospel, and takes long walks in parts of the city not visited at any other time of year. Or an old man rereads *The Power and the Glory* (the book that once brought him back to the church) each year, spends much time in the church and writes once-a-year letters to his grandchildren. Or the pastoral associate puts aside all loose ends of work, takes only the parish's token meals and writes to each of those to be baptized.

In any invitation to keep the Triduum, the tone has a strong enthusiasm: This is what we can expect and even demand of one another. The viewpoint always is first person plural: These are *ours;* these are the things *we* do when *we* assemble in the Triduum. There is nothing of "come and hear the choir" or "come and see the decorations"—leaving the assembly to be an audience.

Beyond this, catechesis can provide suggestions for scripture reading and prayer. The parish can offer publications intended for use in the home (see the bibliography in the appendix, part 4).

Of immense and decisive importance is the example of this keeping of the Triduum: How is the Triduum kept by the clergy, by the parish staff, by persons involved in religious education and the school, by the council and liturgy committee and by others who are visible? This can be discussed without imposing any single practice, but the various ways of fasting that are at the center of Triduum should be publicly aired, especially with those who have this visibility. How the parish comes to keep these days ultimately will have as much to do with example as with preaching and bulletin notices.

These are the types of things that are caught rather than taught. What can happen, year by year, is a growing sense that Lent is going somewhere, toward these three days that are, from beginning to end, in home and at church, all-encompassing, re-creating and simply part of being Catholic.

In this catechesis, we need not campaign against understandings of Holy Week or Triduum that seem not to go beyond a day-by-day memorial of Jesus' last days, death, burial and resurrection. The liturgies themselves, properly celebrated, give the right sense for remembering various moments in the passion, death and resurrection of the Lord. But the liturgies also will manifest the way in which this retelling is caught up in the single mystery as it is proclaimed from the first moment of Holy Thursday when we sing that our glory is the cross.

Those responsible for parish catechesis might ponder this: To what extent do we know that it is baptism that defines us? For most of us, it is still a small extent. Yet without that, without a growing awareness of that most crucial gesture, we can hardly grasp what keeping Lent and observing the paschal fast and the other deeds and disciplines of the Triduum are about. Experience with the RCIA would indicate that a sense for the sacrament of baptism grows in the community through the Vigil liturgy itself, but also through the presence of the catechumens throughout the year, of the elect during Lent, the dismissal of catechumens and elect before the intercessions, and the various rites that mark their relationship to the church. These best teachers can be augmented by preaching and teaching about baptism, but teacher and/or preacher must have it straight. Aidan Kavanagh writes that for each of us there must come to be a memory of our baptism. He argues that there is a

> . . . need for individuals and local churches to have the strongest possible sense of their own Catholic identity, an identity not rooted primarily in their ethnic past or even in the religious rhythms of family and school, *but an identity rooted in the living memory of their own baptism into Christ in his church.* A Christian must have such a memory—whether it derives from regular participation in the baptism of others or, better, from one's own—as both a corrective and an enrichment for all his or her subsequent sacramental encounters. (*The Shape of Baptism,* Pueblo/Liturgical Press, page 176)

In the preparation of the Triduum and in catechesis about the Triduum, there is much that demands attention. The presence of baptism, the way baptism identifies us, is not one item among many. It is the central and defining deed of these days.

Preparing the Liturgy

The rest of this chapter (and the bulk of this book) is addressed to those who are responsible for preparing the parish liturgies during the Triduum. These will be overall matters that should be considered in relation to all that is then said of the particular liturgies of the Triduum.

We are "preparing" the liturgy for the people just as Lent and catechesis are preparing the people for the liturgy. We are not (in Austin Fleming's fine distinction) "planning" the liturgy. That has already been done. The tradition, taking shape in our sacramentary and lectionary and RCIA, has an order, a plan, of liturgy. What is left for us is exactly this work of preparing.

To prepare the liturgy is to make the church's liturgy accessible to the church, this church, right here. To prepare the liturgy is to make it possible for this assembly of baptized people to do what baptism has made their work, their duty and their privilege.

There is a special caution here when the liturgies we speak of happen only once a year. It is so easy for us, even with the Sunday liturgy, to see success and failure in terms of what was done to or for people (they were moved, inspired, made hopeful, informed), rather than in the proper terms: Did this church come here and do its liturgy? With once-a-year liturgies, the temptation to do it for and to people is much stronger. We have insufficient faith in ourselves; we can't believe that we can ask this of one another.

But the first rubric in liturgy preparation is no different for the Triduum: The full, conscious and active participation of the faithful is of the essence; such participation is the right and it is the privilege of the baptized (so forthrightly said by Vatican II in the *Constitution on the Sacred Liturgy*, #14). So every bit of the preparation must be measured in the end by whether—little by little—the church came and did its liturgy.

We need not approach liturgy, then, for what can be put into it or gotten out of it. Rather, we approach these days listening, sniffing, looking, conscious of and in awe of the ways that words and sounds and gestures and tastes and smells can express all the ways we are before our God. Those who prepare do not begin with a blank slate. They begin with the evolving practice of the church. None of us can say what these days are. Together, we hold the ways we have received for keeping these days, ways that are ever in need of scrutiny (but such scrutiny rightly happens only when we know these days extremely well, know them the way good friends and spouses know each other). Too often, people begin with their own notions of what this or that liturgy should be and go on to use the sacramentary and lectionary only where it suits them. An observation from Nathan Mitchell may help to clarify the role of those who prepare:

> The language of worship serves not merely to bless or canonize our experience of the world but to critique and challenge it as well. Liturgy is always an invitation to exceed, to transcend—and even to subvert—the present limits of our experience. For the liturgy operates unabashedly on the principle that there is "always something more"—always something more to our experience of God and world than meets the eye or ear. This is why the most hallowed words of worship are characteristically drawn from sources other than ourselves. (*Assembly,* November 1990)

We approach the liturgies of the Triduum not as several individual problems to be distributed and solved but as one moment that lasts three days, one rite with its private and its public moments. The Vigil is the heart of this and only when it is experienced as such will the other moments of the Triduum come into perspective. No one should be charged with preparing the Holy Thursday liturgy, for example, who has not in experience, study and discussion found how this moment relates to the three days as a whole and to the Vigil in particular.

Those who prepare, first of all, must be thoroughly familiar with the relevant sections of the sacramentary, the lectionary and the RCIA. Even when one has heard the texts and read the rubrics for years, they need to be read anew. This is both preparation of the spirit and of the agenda. Next comes reviewing of the notes and orders of service from the previous year. Then attention can be given to books like this one and to other resources (see the bibliography in the appendix, part 4); these aids to preparation should be used hand in hand with the primary texts of lectionary, sacramentary and RCIA.

As the parish becomes accustomed to celebrating the principal liturgies of the Triduum with great care and participation, those

Gabe Huck notes Austin Fleming's helpful
distinction between our *preparing* the liturgy
and *planning* the liturgy. He asserts the
church & our Tradition have already planned
it; our task is to prepare it — i.e., to make
"accessible" to this local church, at this
specific time.

responsible should become familiar with the celebration of the liturgy of the hours on these days and, in some form, should include these in the way the parish keeps the Triduum. The basic resource, of course, is that volume of *Liturgy of the Hours* that includes the Triduum, but various adaptations of these rites also should be studied. (A chart in the appendix, part 5, will help with setting priorities.)

We know how busy the hours before and between the liturgies of the Triduum have sometimes been. Lists of things to be done get longer: things to find and put in place, practices with ministers, details to be checked. Before approaching the considerations of the Triduum's liturgies that follow in this book, we can make a resolution: "No more!"

Once the Triduum begins, it ought to be a sacred time for everyone. If we are encouraging the elect and the baptized alike to shape their lives on Friday and Saturday around prayer and fasting and the absence of work and entertainment, why do we require something less of ourselves?

Practicing with the ministers for these liturgies is essential, but parishes have shown that the two weekends before the Triduum are possible times for all practicing to take place. Presiders and cantors can repeat this walk-through on Wednesday or Thursday, concentrating on the pace and timing. In the same way, evaluation and suggestions for next year are important, but any discussion of these should wait until Easter Sunday is over.

Part of the readiness of those who prepare the liturgies to put their concerns aside and enter into the Triduum has to do with the room and the objects used. All of the cleaning of the room should be done before Holy Thursday (yes, one can imagine that polishing a candlestick would be a peaceful, contemplative task for a Holy Saturday afternoon—it would be; just be sure to draw the line between that and a crew coming in to scrub and dust). The Triduum begins Holy Thursday night; cleaning the church on Holy Saturday

The Triduum and Ourselves

says, whether we intend it or not, that there's a division between what went before and what comes next. Saturday is for peace and rest; the latter will be needed by all those taking part in the night's vigil.

Those responsible for the arrangement and objects in the room should not feel that each of these days must have its own environment. Each liturgy has particular needs (basin and towels on Thursday night, the cross on Friday), but these are not so many. They are things that are brought forward within the liturgy. The room itself is clean and clear in the beginning and stays that way. It is changed only as the assembly comes and brings a book, basin and towels, bread and wine, the cross, the Easter candle, chrism, incense. The elaborate use of banners, flowers or other decorative materials is best kept for the festive Eastertime.

These days are not glum but they are stark. More than ever, the room needs people to make it "church." The Triduum calls for simplicity and cleanliness of the whole room and for careful selection of each object. That selection, like the rehearsals, is to be done ahead of time so that artists and sacristans may enter into the Triduum without work to be done.

Rehearsals and Other Preparation with the Ministers

It will not do, not in this generation and probably not in the next, simply to "talk through" and call that a rehearsal. That may come first, but there also must be a "walking through." This can happen with the individual ministers or groups of acolytes or communion ministers, but at some point, the whole ensemble must come together and practice as a body. We do not let choirs sing if they do not rehearse, so neither should we let any others perform their ministries without rehearsal. Choirs may separately rehearse sopranos and tenors, but at some point, all must rehearse together. Why do we expect less of those who perform other ministries?

This zeal for rehearsals makes sense only when we accept that the good minister is one who serves the assembly. Such service fails when it is uncertain, self-conscious, showy, entertaining, absent-minded or uncoordinated with other ministries. When that happens, the liturgy ceases to belong to the people. It becomes a set of directions in the hands of the ministers.

Every minister, acolytes included, can have a sense of being at home here, of knowing the order of things. Every minister can have a sense for the liturgy: It is not a random placing of words and gestures, but an order of words and gestures with an integrity. This is not a logic, a mathematics, but a place where I belong, where one deed flows into another. The sense becomes: I know how to do this. Or, even better, one knows how so well that there is no reflection on it at all.

Rehearsals should be in the hands of a person who bears responsibility for the overall coordination of the liturgies of the Triduum. This should be one person, not one for each liturgy. The coordinator works with the chairperson of each ministry to select the ministers and to set the time for rehearsals. It is the coordinator's responsibility to prepare and to know thoroughly the order of service that has been studied by the liturgy board (or whatever the parish authority for this is). The coordinator also prepares schedules and notes for each of the ministries involved. Usually, the coordinator also will prepare the sacramentary for the presider and the detailed orders of service needed by the cantor, instrumentalist and perhaps other key ministers. The sacramentary may be the book used, but more likely it will be a binder (one made suitable for this public use) that contains, in order, all the texts needed by the presider and none that are not needed. Many parishes prepare such books for all major liturgies. After the first year of using this book, the coordinator's task is to make all the changes agreed to.

The order of the liturgy should be firmly set and the details resolved before the main rehearsals. For this to happen, at least in the years when a parish still is working out its order of service for these liturgies, some initial walking through may be needed. Sacristan, presider, musician and coordinator go to the church and work through the uncertainties. The coordinator then incorporates their decisions into the order of service.

At the rehearsals, the coordinator looks out especially for how these ministries will work together in the pace, the back and forth, the details. Much depends on the seemingly trivial. Lack of attention, failure to understand how one role relates to another role: These are the ways that the assembly loses its liturgy. The coordinator is there to see that the liturgy belongs to the assembly. A constant question in the coordinator's mind is: Are we taking this liturgy away from the assembly or making it possible for the assembly to be the subject of the liturgy? Have we thought at each point about the sitting and standing and kneeling of members of the assembly, about their processions and gestures and singing, about the rhythm and sense of the whole?

Also crucial to most of the rehearsals is the sacristan. This ministry often is neglected, to everyone's loss. It is always too much to expect the sacristan and the coordinator to be the same person. The sacristan works closely with the coordinator in studying the order of each service and in preparing notes that apply to the lighting, the furniture, any things that are needed in that liturgy. The sacristan is also in close touch with the environment and art committee in preparing everything that is seen and handled in these liturgies. From year to year, the sacristan keeps detailed records.

The sacristan's participation in the rehearsal sessions helps assure coordination during the Triduum. Respect for the assembly requires that all preparations be made well before the time of the liturgy. From the first moment that members of the assembly begin to arrive, there should be no adjusting of microphones, placement or lighting of candles, or any last-minute instructions to ministers. When all ministers, sacristan and coordinator and presider included, understand themselves first as members of the assembly, and then as serving that assembly in one capacity or another, this becomes clear and natural.

Rehearsals are needed each year, but as a parish sets its own way to keep these days, the music and the movements and the pace of these liturgies do become familiar. We are capable of knowing the once-a-year very well, of looking forward to it and of cherishing it. But it has to be worthy of such anticipation and affection.

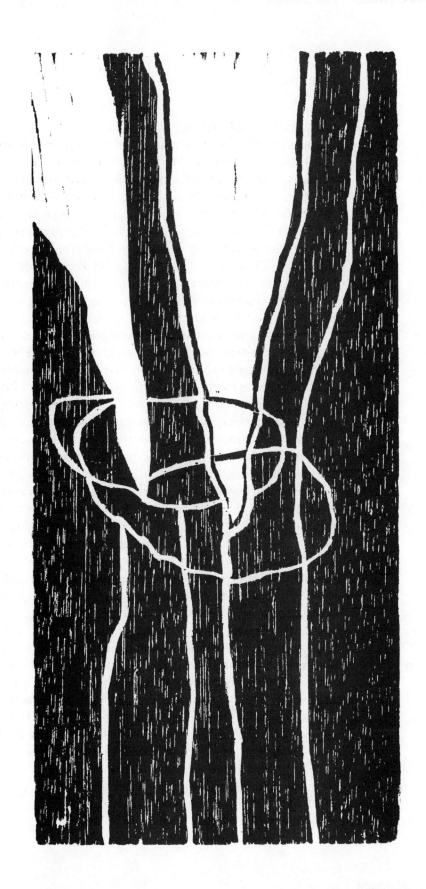

This familiarity gained over the years, however, bears fruit only if rehearsals continue. There always are new ministers.

The best process involves early practicing with the particular ministers. The lectors for the Easter Vigil, for example, come on an early Saturday in Lent for an initial practice and critique. Perhaps the lectors for Holy Thursday and Good Friday are part of this same session or come as it ends. Those who need more work receive a time later in Lent for a further practice. All are asked to return for the main Vigil (or Holy Thursday or Good Friday) rehearsal. That rehearsal, from the lectors' perspective, will be about the order of the night, their places in the assembly, perhaps moving around in the darkness and other practicalities. A few may proclaim their entire reading, but most will do only the first and last lines.

A similar schedule would be set up for the presider, the acolytes, the cantors (who would in any case be practicing, usually with the choir). Each of the three major liturgies would have its own time for the main rehearsal.

The main rehearsals for each liturgy usually can be structured so that those who are needed for only a short time are given a certain time to come and then are free to leave after they have walked through their part. Presider, sacristan, acolytes, cantor and other principal musicians are present throughout. It is their coordination among themselves and with lectors and others that is central to the rehearsal.

To the extent possible, the "real things" should be used at the rehearsal. Practicing with last year's Easter candle, when the new one will be four times as heavy, invites trouble. Practicing the Vigil during the daytime likewise won't work. For the assembly to be well served, ministers have to take these extra measures.

The Presider

The presider cannot be absent from such rehearsals but is to be there both for example and to learn. Even more than other ministers, the presider must know the order of the liturgy by heart. That does not mean memorizing some outline of the Vigil service from a card. It means getting the order of the service into one's muscles and bones, knowing the moment of the Exsultet—what comes before, what follows—the way one knows where to put the verb in a spoken sentence or the way one reaches for the comb after putting the toothbrush away. The danger here is obvious: It sounds like something a robot could do. We've all seen liturgy handled that way. Nothing like that is intended, but there is simply no getting around this: A person is not free to perform a ministry well unless the person has every aspect of it down pat. Then comes freedom to be excellent in the deeds and words of that ministry. Fumbling around and uncertainty and disorder are as ruinous to the assembly's liturgy as presiders who demand all attention on their own wit or piety or bombast.

Each parish is to celebrate these liturgies only once (this is itself a key to understanding both parish and liturgy). If there is more than one priest in the parish, two questions arise. First, for the eucharist on Holy Thursday and the eucharist of the Vigil, should there be concelebration? Arguments can be made for and against. Should the decision be to have concelebration, this is to be done in the simplest manner possible (e.g., the concelebrants remaining throughout with the assembly). There can be no question of any type of concelebration for the liturgy of Good Friday; additional clergy simply are part of the assembly. Second, should there be a rotation of presiders during these liturgies? Some have found that the unity of the days is enhanced when the pastor presides at all of the major assemblies. Others see value in the pastor presiding only at the Vigil: This gives the Vigil a preeminence. However the parish decides this question, all clergy in the parish as well as members of the staff should be present at these liturgies. This is part of the example discussed earlier.

Participation Aids

This problem is not that different from the Sunday liturgy. Parishes that rely on some form of monthly or seasonal booklet prepared by others, the missalette approach, will be tempted to use these books for the Triduum. Such aids reinforce the perception that the people are spectators. They follow the program with a booklet. If what we are about these three days is taken seriously, if there is something to this baptizing and confirming and sharing eucharist, then surely it is not to end with the Christian's eyes glued to a missalette. A parish that works with the lectors and presiders and cantors does not need to have the written text in every person's hands. The word is lively when it is heard and its speaker or singer seen.

The order and the gestures of these liturgies, when they are as well formed and well paced as possible in any parish, do not need to be written down for all to follow. They speak for themselves. Writing them down and placing them in every person's hands is itself a violation of all we hope to be about here. It alters everything because it fails to understand and so respect the assembly.

Like all our liturgy, the rites of the Triduum are chanted and sung. That is how people do liturgy. Most of the music of these liturgies is not needed in every hand. We sing acclamations, refrains, litanies. These are picked up from a cantor and sung from memory; we do this naturally at the Vigil when we sing the psalm refrains in the darkness. A printed handout or hymnal is needed only for the occasional hymn. If the parish has a hymnal, then it is there for the few times it is needed. If the parish has no hymnal, then every effort should be made to prepare a simple but dignified booklet. Paper for the cover and for the body of the booklet, typefaces, layout and art should all be attended to; these booklets are as much a part of the liturgy as any other object. Any shabbiness or carelessness brings a message. Having the needed music for all three liturgies (and perhaps Vespers on Easter) in a single booklet strengthens the sense for the unity of these days. Such a booklet might include a very simple outline of each liturgy along with the necessary music in place.

The Schedule

Well in advance of the Triduum, a schedule is ordinarily published in the parish. This also is an opportunity for catechesis. The form and the information given would evolve from year to year. In some cases, it might be printed and mailed to parishioners. The schedule could be printed with prayers to be used at home on the back (see *Catholic Household Blessings and Prayers* for examples of texts and a format for prayers).

The schedule can reinforce both the unity and the flow of the Triduum. It can be inviting in appearance, tone and vocabulary, conveying a sense that everything else comes to a standstill and that the parish is gathered almost continually during this time. The example in the appendix, part 6, shows that the schedule can offer a simple order of service for each of the three main liturgies.

This final introductory word is about that element of our liturgy that, even when much else is faulty, can convey how thoroughly the liturgy is to be the work of the assembly. Those who prepare the music of these liturgies must follow a number of principles:

The Music

First, as in all our liturgy, rite and music are one. We do not sing during the liturgy, we sing the liturgy. Thus, the choices of text and tune are rooted in a knowledge and deep understanding of these rites.

Second, the liturgy is sung by the assembly with the help of cantor, choir and (only as needed to accompany until the eucharist of the Vigil) instrumentalists. There must be continuity from year to year so that the assembly knows what the washing of the feet sounds like, what the adoration of the cross sounds like. Then it can be theirs.

Third, the Triduum is sung beginning on Holy Thursday and ending at Easter Vespers. These are not a number of concerts, each with its own program. There is one rite here, stretching over the three days. It is natural to repeat, to develop and to build. The communion song of Thursday can be heard during communion of the Vigil. The quiet ostinato that ends the time in assembly on Thursday can be sung quietly before the beginning of Friday's liturgy and once more as the assembly begins to disperse. Some of Lent's psalms or communion refrains will be heard in these days as will some of the tunes that will define Eastertime. Various hymns and antiphons bind together all the celebrations of the liturgy of the hours.

One temptation will be the great amount of music written. Music directors may search for the best but should be wary of replacing anything in the parish's accustomed Triduum music that is being sung well by the assembly. Even more important as a criterion for retaining music that is well sung or substituting a new piece that is likely to be well sung: Does this composition, in word and in tune, make a marriage with the rite itself so that music and rite are not two but one?

There is sometimes a temptation to leave the assembly out, turning various parts over to the choir. An hour of "sacred song" at some point during these days (not joined to any of the rites) may not always be out of place, but it is out of place to rob the assembly of the way they are to sing this liturgy.

Some day, in many parishes, the music that the assembly sings will be a major factor in the memory of and eagerness for the Triduum. We will hum sturdy tunes for weeks of Eastertime. We will look forward to the Alleluia just because it is so beautiful and magnificent when it bursts forth again. We will associate the washing of the feet with some lovely tune and text, and we will have been introduced to new facets of the cross through the tunes and texts that come back each year, not exhausted but so full that they can carry the church for generations. The music has to be that good and be that much given to the assembly.

Entering: The Liturgy of Holy Thursday Night

Lent has no "moment" of conclusion. Lent is over when, on Thursday night, we enter the Easter Triduum. What we do have near the end of Lent, however, are two traditional actions that allow the Triduum to begin. One of these has been maintained and one only now is being revived.

Chrism Mass

The Chrism Mass of Holy Thursday (that is, Holy Thursday as the final day of Lent) gathers the diocesan church to consecrate the oil that will be used in each parish church to anoint the newly baptized at the Vigil. For various reasons, this rite often is separated from these last moments of Lent and located earlier in the week or even in the previous week. Two things seem important here. First, the Chrism Mass is the single regular moment that draws the entire diocese (not only the clergy) together around the bishop. Both for those who participate and for those who do not there should be a wide awareness that this is happening. Second, the focus of this liturgy is the blessing and consecration of these oils so that they may be used throughout this local church, and particularly the focus is the holy chrism that will be used everywhere in the Triduum that is about to begin. As often happens, various emphases from time to time have added other baggage to the Chrism Mass, baggage it does not bear well. In some dioceses, efforts now are made to let the Chrism Mass be the strongest possible sign of the local church, gathered around its bishop, to prepare the fragrant oil that very soon will seal the baptisms of new Christians.

Reconciliation

At one period, the reconciliation of public penitents was done on Holy Thursday so that the church might be made whole and so come to Easter. These penitents had been solemnly expelled from the church at the beginning of Lent and had been seen doing penance for these 40 days. In our day, all that remained of this was the practice of confession and communion during Lent and Easter-time. From the time communal penance services became part of our ritual during the 1970s, parishes began celebrating these near the end of Lent. This practice is encouraged in the 1988 Vatican *Circular Letter.* Regarding penitential services, it says:

> It is advantageous that Lent be concluded both for the individual Christian and for the entire community with some sort of penitential service as a preparation for a fuller participation in the paschal mystery. This service should take place before the Easter Triduum, but should not immediately precede the evening Mass of the Lord's Supper. (#37)

Some parishes have gone further in exploring what the restoration of an order of penitents might be in these times. Usually, these parishes have a reconciliation of penitents near the end of Lent (sometimes as part of the Holy Thursday evening liturgy). In some places, the practice is to begin Lent with the confession of sins and the taking on of penitential disciplines, and to conclude Lent with the ritual celebration of God's mercy.

In general, any form of reconciliation at the end of Lent should not be associated with the rite of accepting baptized persons into full communion with the Roman Catholic Church. The timing of the latter is sometimes a problem, but this reception into full communion is best not confused with repentance and forgiveness and has little to do with concluding Lent.

Because this book does not deal with Lent or its liturgies, these reconciliation rites will not be discussed here. They do not belong to the Triduum itself. The same is to be said for individual celebrations of the rite of reconciliation; they should be completed before the Triduum begins, though the church's discipline at this time still allows confessions during the Triduum.

As a church, we have been unable to recover a practice of the sacrament of reconciliation. The efforts described concerning the order of penitents during Lent are one effort to find something of how to do reconciliation today. We need the rituals of penance and of reconciliation, but we cannot invent them whole and many of the understandings and practices of the past have long lost their symbolic power. Catholic assemblies in this culture do not seem to have the basic vocabulary to speak (in language or in symbol) of God's love, of the great power of evil in our world and lives, of the struggle we have and the victory, too, in Christ. When we try, our language and our ritual often become too soft, too individualistic or too global. Perhaps it is a matter of humility, of keeping our eyes wide open to our world, of reflection, of study and of patience. Some things cannot be forced, but neither can we ignore such matters if we live under the gospel.

Perhaps all that we can ask is that the conclusion of Lent bring simple rites in which we can express the repentance that we have sought throughout Lent and can receive assurance of God's mercy to the sinner. For this, the *Rite of Penance* should be studied thoroughly to shape parish practice; it includes a sample lenten penitential service. With this, however, should come a thorough-going appreciation for the reconciling that fairly bursts from the ritual deeds of the Triduum: the washing of one another's feet, the kissing of the cross, the common fast and, most perfectly, the paschal eucharist of the Vigil.

The *General Norms for the Liturgical Year and the Calendar* puts it simply: "The Easter Triduum begins with the evening Mass of the Lord's Supper, reaches its high point in the Easter Vigil and closes with Evening Prayer on Easter Sunday" (#19). There is one ritual here; it has a beginning, a climax and a conclusion.

That beginning is tonight's liturgy. Before all else, the liturgy of Holy Thursday evening is entrance into these three days. Before we think about tonight as the night we wash feet, or the night we process with the Blessed Sacrament, or the night we commemorate the Last Supper, before all of this, we see this night as the first movement of the Easter Triduum. That means taking great care that the celebration of this night's liturgy does not isolate itself, cut Thursday off from the rest of the days. It means being strict in

Knowing the Evening Liturgy on Holy Thursday

judging any additions to this liturgy that would define Holy Thursday apart from its relation to the whole time until Sunday afternoon. Most especially, this liturgy and this night need no additions in the form of "commitment rites" or of elements that attempt to imitate the Passover seder. Our "commitment rite" comes at the side of the font during the Vigil. Our Passover is the whole rite of these three days. We can well profit from the Jewish seder, but in the company of Jews as they celebrate their festival.

The preparation of the liturgy begins with reading and reflecting on the texts, taking time to let the language settle in. We have to hear the same old words and the same old tunes and the same old gestures. That is, of course, the source of their power, that they have come year in and year out, that we can see them from all different sides and almost always from a side we never before imagined. "Glory in the cross," "Do you wash my feet?" or "You are proclaiming the death of the Lord"—they shock us with the depth and dimensions of this night. The words, the gestures, the songs, when all are done by those who have tried to keep Lent, when done with the once-a-year dignity they deserve, can draw all into the Triduum. The deeds of this night are to make a beginning.

The Time of the One Liturgy

The first day of the Triduum goes from sunset on Thursday to sunset on Friday. This is the sixth day, the day when God formed us from clay and breath. The church has long likened Jesus to this Adam: Today on the cross, Jesus sleeps as Adam did, and from the sleeper's side comes the church, the new Eve. On the day when the first creation was completed, we celebrate the new creation. In another paradise, we approach another tree of life, the cross.

Understood as an evening-to-evening day, the first day of the Triduum, the liturgy of Holy Thursday is celebrated in the evening. The sacramentary allows that the Ordinary may permit this liturgy to be celebrated on Thursday morning, but only for those "who are in no way able to take part in the evening Mass." A parish would have to ponder long on "in no way" before deciding on a morning Mass, or on any second Mass at all. Sometimes, the morning Mass has been celebrated with schoolchildren; it hardly could be said that they are "in no way" able to attend the parish liturgy in the evening. Better to celebrate with the children some farewell to Lent on Thursday morning and to invite them to come with their parents in the evening. Only when the crowds have to be turned away on Holy Thursday evening or afternoon is there occasion to think of adding a second liturgy—or moving to a larger space.

What is the reasoning here? If we want to involve people in the Triduum, wouldn't it make more sense to offer Masses at all likely times to get as many people as possible to attend? That is the attitude that has led us to multiply weekend Masses: the dictates of convenience. It is a matter of how we think about the assembly of the baptized: Is it so many individuals with all their various motives for being present at a time that happened to suit the schedule of each, or is it this church, this assembly of the baptized who do the eucharist every Lord's Day? The latter has not recently been our Roman Catholic way. Obligation somehow led us to convenience. Those who are told they must come are used to having Mass at various convenient times. The notion of church is lost to the notion of the individual. The notion that the liturgy is the deed of this assembly, this particular church gathering every Lord's Day, is lost to the notion that Mass is something to "go to" or "attend."

Here in the Triduum, the rubrics express a notion of being the church that our Sundays could well imitate. They do this with such a simple thing as the rule about one liturgy in a parish. Do we want people to attend this liturgy? Absolutely. Will we therefore make it convenient? No, because convenience plays no role whatsoever in these days. "Convenience" would imply that this deed, the liturgy, has to fit in with other deeds of normal life. But beginning tonight, the church's presumption is that normal life for church people ceases. If we have here a parish, then these rubrics say: All should be together! Together we will do this Triduum or not at all. The rubrics say: What happens here is done by the church. So assemble the church and get on with it. The rubrics say: Do everything possible to have everyone under one roof at one time.

The time of this night's liturgy should be such that it allows people to take first a supper that we should come to understand as the last real meal until we finish with the Vigil. In some parishes, this has taken the form of a simple communal meal, potluck or prepared by some parish organization, at 6:00 PM or a little later, followed by the liturgy at 7:30. Where there has been a weekly parish "fasting" supper (bread and soup and money for the hungry) during Lent, this is simply the last of these.

Parishes now seem to understand why a meal or even a social hour following the liturgy tonight is not in keeping with what it is we have begun: the paschal fast. Clergy, staff and all involved in liturgical ministries should give the example tonight by dispersing quietly or remaining in prayer, but with no chatter and no socializing.

The Flow of the Liturgy

We begin our approach to the liturgy itself with its overall movement. There is a "see the forest before the trees" rule in working with the liturgy.

The introductory rites of the evening liturgy (and so of the whole Triduum) begin in our strange glory, the cross: "We should glory in the cross of our Lord Jesus Christ, for he is our salvation, our life and our resurrection; through him we are saved and made free." Galatians 6:14 stands in the sacramentary as the keynote to the whole Triduum—no separation here of cross and resurrection, of suffering and glory. No wonder the ringing of bells marked the opening moments of this liturgy: The church gathers to enter the Triduum, to glory in the cross.

So gathered, the assembly listens to three stories: the Passover event, Paul's account of the Last Supper, John's account of the washing of the feet. There is much here that needs excellent proclamation, ample silence, psalmody and homily. Then, before the catechumens are dismissed and the assembly joins in the intercessions, the mandatum takes place. This is washing feet, the Lord's command (in Latin, *mandatum,* and thus our word "Maundy" Thursday).

The preparation of the gifts on this day is to be more than setting the table and taking up the collection. The offerings on a normal Sunday are "for the church or the poor" (*General Instruction of the Roman Missal*, #49). But today the sacramentary says: "At the beginning of the liturgy of the eucharist, there may be a procession of the faithful with gifts for the poor." We find no mention of gifts for the church, but rather the clearest gesture of what this church is: We are for the life of the world. That's all.

After all of this, the liturgy of the eucharist is quiet. This may seem strange, but it becomes clear in light of the character of the Triduum itself where the eucharist of the Vigil stands as climax to the fasting, vigiling and rites of initiation. Our eucharistic liturgy on Thursday night is sober, without special singing or music. This is not a night to embellish either the text or the music of the eucharistic prayer or the communion rite. These rites should contain no play-acting of the Last Supper. The communion rite, with communion from both bread and cup, should have the same quiet seriousness as the eucharistic prayer. After communion, there is solemnity in the procession to the tabernacle (clearly intended to be in another space), but this procession is without any texts before or after, only the words of the hymn.

This conclusion is noteworthy. Blessings and dismissals normally conclude our liturgies. But here the presumption is that the assembly continues — and on Friday there will be no call to worship of any kind, and again no dismissal. Again, the rubrics are showing us the wholeness of these days. Parishes that have had the custom of refreshments and a social hour after this liturgy should reconsider such practices. All this good effort can be directed toward the true "break fast" that follows the Vigil.

A liturgy like that of Holy Thursday night needs only to be done well. It does not need embellishment. It is a lengthy liturgy by Roman Catholic standards, but it has a rhythm that can carry it. There is much movement: the entrance itself, the washing of feet, the dismissal of the catechumens, the gifts for the poor, communion, the procession to the tabernacle.

The liturgy is complex enough to invite confusion if the whole is not well thought out and rehearsed. Because of the length, the change in tone after the catechumens are dismissed is helpful and important.

The Place and Objects Needed

The room where the assembly gathers has been prepared, but prepared for the church to enter the Triduum. Perhaps to carry this through would mean no furniture, no anything. In these next three days, we stand without distraction. We are without the lovely distractions of paintings, sculpture, banners, flowers. We look like what we are: people in between worlds and times, finished with the disciplines of Lent but not yet prepared to approach the font of baptism, stripped down to essentials so that we can at last remember again what the essentials are.

At the very least, all the superfluous furniture and other clutter found in most churches should have been removed: flags and their stands, candles and candle stands that are not used, chairs and kneelers, vases and microphones and music stands. Freeing from clutter applies not only to the area around the altar but to the whole room, including the entrance areas and the outside. If special participation aids are to be used instead of the hymnals or missalettes, then the latter should be removed altogether. Note also that the rubrics call for the tabernacle to be empty. If the church's tabernacle is located within the main worship area (not the norm established by the various documents on the place for the eucharistic assembly), then the tabernacle lamp is one more piece of furniture that can be removed. Holy water fonts are empty and are removed or covered.

The bread for today should receive the same attention as the bread for any Sunday. Sometimes, however, these days are a way to begin practices that then can spread to Sundays. That would mean using large loaves, baked locally. Enough bread must be prepared for the communion today and tomorrow. The temptation may be to use the locally baked bread for today and to consecrate the wafers for Friday's liturgy. But the directives (e.g., "The nature of the sign demands that the material for the eucharistic celebration truly have the appearance of food," *General Instruction,* #283) make no exceptions for Good Friday. Most of the breads that parishes now prepare for the eucharist will stay fresh if tightly wrapped when they are placed in the tabernacle. The wine should not be anything out of the ordinary, given the simplicity of tonight's eucharist.

If the parish has more than one set of plates and cups, the more ordinary set might be used tonight and the others at the Vigil. The lectionary, however, both tonight and Friday and at the Vigil, should be the finest. Other vessels will be needed for the washing of the feet; these should be large, workable vessels, not plastic. Let the vessels themselves show respect for the tender work they serve.

The vessels for the holy oils also are seen tonight (see the following for their possible presence in the liturgy). Because the oils differ in their function and the amount a parish uses of each, their vessels should differ also. In any case, these vessels should be given the same attention and beauty as those that hold the bread and wine.

The Entrance Rite

An entrance rite is always about the entrance of the assembly into its liturgy. The purpose of the entrance rite is to form individuals into the community that does this liturgy and to ready that community to hear the word of God and celebrate the eucharist.

Tonight is a night of entrance. Though the liturgy will end in great quiet, the arrival of the assembly should be a time of joyful greeting and of excitement about what now is to begin. The church bells might ring all during the time people are assembling and through the opening hymn of the liturgy, then become silent with the invitation, "Let us pray." Great attention will be on the elect who now enter the final hours of preparation for baptism.

The procession of ministers and the hymn is one element in this entrance rite. Ideally, the whole assembly would join in this procession, singing and moving together into the church. If this is not happening, the usual ministers might be joined by one or two ministers carrying thuribles filled with incense, by the choir, by those who will have their feet washed (who could carry in and put in place all the vessels and towels to be used in the washing of the feet), by the newly reconciled penitents, by those carrying the holy oils. A solemn procession could move down all the aisles at once, thus embracing the whole assembly in such an entrance. All those who process join in the song. Most of them then go to their places in the assembly.

The presider might call the assembly to worship even before the procession, speaking from the front or the back of the room. (The presider could well be in place, in front, waiting with others who arrive early for the congregation to assemble and for the liturgy to begin. When the time comes, the presider stands and gestures for all to stand.) From the front or from the procession itself, the presider begins with the sign of the cross and greeting and any brief comment, concluding with some invitation to enter now into the Triduum. For example:

> My sisters and brothers, we have completed the 40 days of Lent and so (now let us rise and) let us enter into this Paschal Triduum. Let us receive into our midst this Easter Three Days, celebrating the Lord's passion and resurrection and moving toward the font of baptism, the anointing with chrism and the table of the eucharist.

As will be suggested in what follows, the entrance verse from Galatians given in the sacramentary could be spoken also by the presider to conclude this call to worship.

The processional song begins at once. The procession usually would wait through most of one verse, then begin slowly moving through the assembly. If the presider is in front, the minister carrying the lectionary would come last in the procession and those with the oils immediately precede the book. An acolyte with a candle could walk beside or just in front of each person carrying one of the vessels of oil. The procession should be well spaced. Most of those in it (e.g., those to have their feet washed) come to the front, bow to the altar and take their places in the assembly. All those who have nothing else in their hands carry the participation aid and join in singing.

The first singing of tonight can do much to create the sense of assembly, of prayer together. It has to come strongly from the assembly. The tendency still is to select a hymn with a eucharistic theme, thus supporting a "historical" approach to this night's liturgy: Holy Thursday is about the Last Supper. This misses the larger sense of the Triduum. The text provided in the sacramentary for the entrance rite, quoted earlier, does not go astray but is in tune with our solemn entrance into the whole of the three days:

> We should glory in the cross of our Lord Jesus Christ, for he is our salvation, our life and our resurrection; through him we are saved and made free. (Galatians 6:14)

That is exactly the entrance to the Triduum. It is a text that grasps the whole. The church is not afraid to speak of glory and of cross, knowing both and that the two are one. The church can sing at this first moment of "our resurrection."

A first suggestion then is that these words be heard tonight. They could be spoken by the presider immediately after the greeting and the sign of the cross. In this case, both the call to worship and this text should be committed to memory and spoken strongly and directly. The hymn should be intoned exactly as the last words, "made free," are concluded.

A second suggestion is that the hymn's text and music echo this crucial text. There is one text that particularly captures this sense and has a long association with these days. The text is given here for the reader to see it anew and consider its use:

> Sing, my tongue, the song of triumph,
> Tell the story far and wide;
> Tell of dread and final battle,
> Sing of Savior crucified,
> How upon the cross a victim
> Vanquishing in death he died.
>
> He endured the nails, the spitting,
> Vinegar and spear and reed;
> From that holy body broken
> Blood and water forth proceed:
> Earth and stars and sky and ocean
> By that flood from stain are freed.
>
> Faithful Cross, above all other,
> One and only noble tree,
> None in foliage, none in blossom,
> None in fruit your peer may be;
> Sweet the wood and sweet the iron
> And your load, most sweet is he.
>
> Bend your boughs, O Tree of glory!
> All your rigid branches, bend!
> For a while the ancient temper
> That your birth bestowed, suspend;
> And the King of earth and heaven
> Gently on your bosom tend.

This sixth-century hymn knows how glory and cross are one mystery in our lives and in the baptism we have received; it is about the Passover mystery of Christ who has become our Passover. It can be sung with the same tune as the other "Pange Lingua" that concludes this day's liturgy (the hymn by Thomas Aquinas), or to another tune in this meter. The tune chosen should be one to move by, a tune to enter by. Other texts may come even closer, in a given assembly, to giving voice to the entrance to our Passover.

There is a question about carrying the cross in this procession. Because the veneration of the cross is the central moment of the Good Friday liturgy, some would question the presence of the cross in today's liturgy. No answer seems entirely logical, but liturgy often has its own logic. That the cross is carried at the head of our processing into the Triduum seems proper. What then? On Sundays, the cross in place in the midst of the congregation signifies that the church has assembled. So the cross could go to its usual place. Perhaps it then would make sense to leave it there through the Triduum, right into Sunday—if this is the cross to be venerated on Friday (in which case the "unveiling" option never would be chosen). If this is not the cross to be venerated, then it can be carried at the head of the procession to the tabernacle after this evening's liturgy and be left there until it is needed for the liturgies of Sunday morning (note that the cross is not carried in the procession from the fire at the Vigil; the paschal candle leads that procession).

If the newly blessed and consecrated oils are carried in the procession, their presence in this church should be hailed. This can be done in the following manner (presuming that the sign of the cross, greeting and invitation have occurred before the hymn): When the ministers carrying the three vessels have finished the procession, they turn and face the assembly until the hymn is concluded. The minister carrying the lectionary remains within the assembly, also facing the three ministers. A text has been published by the Bishops' Committee on the Liturgy in the United States that can be used or adapted. One at a time, each of the three ministers steps forward, holds up the vessel of oil and says:

This oil of the sick has been blessed by our bishop for the healing of body, mind and soul. May the sick, who are anointed with it, experience the compassion of Christ and his saving love.

This oil of catechumens has been blessed by our bishop for the anointing of those preparing for baptism. Through this anointing they are strengthened by Christ to resist the power of Satan and reject evil in all its forms, as they prepare for the saving waters of baptism.

This holy chrism, a mixture of olive oil and perfume, has been consecrated by our bishop and the priests of our diocese. It will be used to anoint infants after baptism, those who are to be confirmed, bishops and priests at their ordination and altars and churches at the time of their dedication.

Perhaps the presentation of the chrism could read: "After the elect are baptized in our midst at the Easter Vigil, they will be anointed with this fragrant oil in confirmation. It also will be used to anoint infants after baptism, to anoint bishops and priests at their ordination, and to anoint altars and churches at the time of their dedication."

All of this can be done within the movement of the entrance rite as long as it does not become complex and drawn out. If, for example, the ministers would have a difficult time approaching a microphone, it would be best to have another person proclaim the announcement of the oils; each person holding a vessel would step forward and elevate the vessel during the time that the oil is being heralded.

Then the three ministers take their vessels to the ambry (if it is in full view) or to a place prepared near the font or the altar. When the vessels are in place, the presider honors the holy oils and the altar itself with incense. The song can resume as soon as the oils have been announced and can continue until the incensation is finished. Verses are added or repeated so that the music unifies the whole entrance rite. Incense can, if desired, be used in the gospel procession and certainly will be used in the final procession to the tabernacle.

The oils should not disappear after tonight, never to be seen until renewed a year from now. If the ambry is not in a public place, then perhaps during Eastertime the sacred chrism can be given a place of honor near the font.

What of the penitential rite and of the Gloria today? Given the way this liturgy comes after Lent and given the way it serves as entrance to the Triduum, one could argue (based on the various documents that speak of elements within the entrance rites) that the penitential rite should be omitted and that a decision about the Gloria should take into account the parish tradition. If "Sing, my tongue, the song of triumph" or something of this sense has become the way this parish enters into tonight's liturgy, then a second song (the Gloria) in the entrance rite is perhaps superfluous. On the other hand, if the parish places great importance on the singing of the Gloria today, with the bells ringing inside and outside the church, then perhaps the Gloria itself might be the entrance song. The order then could be: The presider (from the front or back, before the procession) proclaims the invitation, sign of the cross, greeting and "We should glory . . ." as described previously. Instead of the hymn, the Gloria would accompany the procession. The setting of the Gloria selected should be one in which all can join; it is not to be a piece for choir alone. Settings such as Peloquin's "Gloria of the Bells" provide for assembly, choir and cantor. After the singing and procession, the entrance rite would conclude with the announcement of the oils and putting them in place with incensation (the refrain of the Gloria might be repeated) and the opening prayer.

The practice of the church for many centuries was that musical instruments were not used between the Gloria of Holy Thursday and the Gloria of the Vigil. Rubrics (in the *Circular Letter,* for example, #50) say that instruments are to be used during this time "only to sustain the singing." This is, in fact, one form of our fasting during the first two days of the Triduum. This fasting is from richness and embellishment. We are holding our breath, waiting, excited. The festivity of Eastertime must wait for the Triduum to reach its high point (and even at the Vigil, there is a certain restraint). So for these two days, instruments are not used to embellish (though one can imagine how a simple flute solo between sung parts during the mandatum is not embellishing but is fully in the spirit of this "fast"). The music budget can be better used to employ extra instrumentalists on Easter and the Sundays of Easter than during these days.

If the Gloria is not sung, the presider invites "Let us pray" as soon as the song is completed and all who have been involved in the procession are in their places. After a time of silence, the presider proclaims the opening prayer. The text of the opening prayer in the sacramentary is not particularly strong. The former collect in the Roman Missal, though it has other problems, has in many ways a better sense for this moment:

> O God, you punished Judas for his crime and rewarded the penitent thief's faith. Be merciful to us; and as our Lord Jesus Christ in his passion gave to each according to their deserts, so may we be given the grace to rise again with him, freed from our former sin.

The oration from Evening Prayer on Holy Thursday also has a larger approach:

> Father, for your glory and our salvation you appointed Jesus Christ eternal High Priest. May the people he gained for you by his blood come to share in the power of his cross and resurrection by celebrating his memorial in this eucharist, for he lives and reigns. . . .

The Scriptures

From this first moment until the end of the Triduum, the scriptures are altogether too much for us. Again and again, the assembly opens its book of scriptures to powerful poetry and stories. But it is all up to those who read the scriptures aloud to the assembly. Those who read from the Hebrew Scriptures or from the letters of the New Testament should be the finest lectors the parish has. Even so, they—along with those who read the gospels—should attend required practice sessions. The agenda at these sessions is, first, to have the lectors see the power and depth of their readings, then to speak them so that this will be heard by the assembly. The problem often is our inability as readers to hear and to be stunned by these texts. They can seem dull, so familiar, without spark—and then they are read that way. Preparation is mostly about unveiling.

The first time that we open our book in the Triduum it is to Exodus 12: "The Lord said to Moses and Aaron in the land of Egypt, 'This month shall be for you the beginning of months.'" It is a reading of rubrics: the tenth day . . . if the household is too small for a lamb . . . take some of the blood and put it on the two door-posts . . . your sandals on your feet. And rubrics generally are not a good read. But here is one of the foundation stories. Here is the bound-up people getting ready, getting dressed in fact, to leave the land of oppression. Here is that animal, a lamb. And here is blood. And here is night. And here is the essential core that got us here: "When I see the blood, I will pass over you." A reader needs to marvel at the nouns and verbs of this reading and how they come together, has to want others then to hear them—not made fancy or overly dramatic, but made as astounding as they are.

The second reading is short and so needs a slow pace in its telling. It builds not to the words of Jesus to his disciples but to Paul's last line to the Corinthians: "As often as you eat this bread and drink the cup, you proclaim the Lord's death until he comes." It might be spoken in a number of ways, so long as we hear what is being said. Like the earlier reading, here is blood as life and death, blood as bond between us, eating as some type of proclamation, and all of this in a world where there is something to be accomplished. It is no easy matter for a lector to grapple with the words that have been so tamed, and even more difficult, in the few seconds it takes to read these, for that lector to engage the church itself in this struggle.

The gospel reading today, as the passion tomorrow, is from the gospel of John. It, too, is about this passover, and the event it narrates is a ritual, a foot washing, a tiny story that for us has gathered up this great passage of Christ and how close it is to our own existence. In a story so dangerously familiar, the way to have it heard (first by the reader, then by all) is not in dramatic narrative of the story and dialogue, as if telling it to those who have not heard it before. Rather, it will be heard when the reader is past familiarity and engaged with the mystery that is being told here. A reader must want to engage this assembled church as the reader is engaged. The reader is stunned with the words and notions: "loved his own who were in the world," "girded himself with a towel," "you shall never!" and "if I have washed your feet." And the reader wants to break through to the church here with the way those words are how we baptized people grasp this world. The reader has nothing new to add to the story—except what it means for this church at this moment.

In this as in every liturgy, haste can ruin good effort. The liturgy of the word must have the fine pace that the parish should know from its Sunday liturgies, perhaps today a bit more contemplative. Pace is crucial. Silence should follow the first two readings, at least a full minute for each. The psalm that follows the first reading should allow for participation of the assembly in the refrain.

The homily follows the reading of the gospel. The rubric in the sacramentary sounds like a compromise between two understandings of today's liturgy. It speaks of the homily as "explaining" the principal mysteries commemorated in this Mass: institution of eucharist and priesthood and Christ's command to love one another. It is better to have preaching from the scriptures we have just heard, preaching that, probably without mentioning the mandatum, prepares us exactly for the glorious business of washing feet.

The Mandatum

The washing of the feet, as it is to be done in our churches, is not a dramatization of the gospel story. Certainly there is a way in which this deed and the gospel and the homily are in conversation. But the mandatum is not to be done during the gospel nor is it to be done in a manner that tries to reenact the gospel story (with costume, dialogue, setting). To do so is to limit, to imprison the rite within a drama. The drama of a reenactment, if well done, can clearly be something moving and full of insight. But that is another type of task than the one the church has in mind here. Our efforts are rather to let this deed, this ritual, have all the ambiguity and all the power it can.

In this regard, note that in the sacramentary this rite has no words except the words that are sung by the assembly. This happens several times during the Triduum: a ritual with no words for presider or other minister. This should be given a thoroughgoing respect. We need add no words. Let the gesture and the song speak for themselves as the church's sacramentary believes that they can.

The mandatum is a once-a-year deed. To do it well, to do it so that it involves the entire assembly, requires that the ministers thoroughly know everything they are to do. This does not mean some type of perfection; things will go wrong. But when the work is being done by persons who have rehearsed and who have prepared themselves with reflection on what they are doing, then the mistakes will be taken in stride by everyone—like forgetting to put the napkins around at a dinner party. We are at home in this activity and we can take in stride a mistake or omission. When the deed is taken as casual, or as walking through some directions on the page, or especially as a dramatic reenactment of the Upper Room, then the mistakes create even greater gaps between the assembly and the ministers. So much depends on the sense presider and ministers have for whether we have an audience and performers or an assembly and its ministers.

There have been various ways of both doing and understanding the mandatum. Seen simply as something our church does on this night and at no other time in the year, it serves almost as a keynote of the Triduum, a proclamation: Here is what these days are about, washing feet and having our feet washed. In such a deed can be found—for it is to mirror the everyday ways of people being with one another—the mundane meaning of our passover in Christ.

The mandatum may or may not be related in history to early practices (third century) where the elect were told to wash themselves on the Thursday before the Saturday night when they were baptized. By Augustine's time in North Africa, the bishop was washing the feet of those to be baptized and of other members of the assembly (see *Jerusalem Revisited* by Kenneth Stevenson, Liturgical Press, page 38). In any case, for us there is some association of this gesture and the baptisms to come. This was said well in the third century by Origen:

> Jesus, come, my feet are dirty. You have become a servant for my sake, so fill your basin with water; come, wash my feet. I know that I am bold in saying this, but your own words have made me fearful: "If I do not wash your feet, you will have no companionship with me." Wash my feet, then, so that I may be your companion. But what am I saying; "Wash my feet"? Peter could say these words, for all that needed washing were his feet. For the rest, he was completely clean. I must be made clean with that other washing of which you said: "I have a baptism with which I must be baptized."

Washing feet, the cross, baptism: This author knew how such are expressions of a life caught up in this passing over on which we have entered. The words of Jesus, "I have a baptism," from Luke 12:50, look toward the cross as does all baptism, as does this tiny deed of kneeling down and washing another's feet or sitting down and letting my feet be washed.

The mandatum takes place before the elect are dismissed. It speaks for itself of the church, of the cross, of what awaits us.

Until recently, those parishes that maintained the mandatum generally had the pastor wash 12 feet, one on each of a dozen men. It now has become more common to make this a broader action. Those whose feet are washed usually represent the whole spectrum of the parish: men and women, all ages (including children), persons involved in the parish and persons not involved, persons manifesting all the diversity the parish has—racially, ethnically, economically and politically, too (including parishioners whose views of the church are likely to be conflicting; barefoot, the differences are different).

Some discussion about whether women are included has, in the United States at least, been resolved by the Bishops' Committee on the Liturgy; they noted that this is an established custom, that it expresses the reality of our lives and should be maintained. Gerard Sloyan has asked of the mandatum that it be a meaningful symbol of service:

> What will symbolize this best, not as between pastor and people, but among people who are on an absolute par in their call to service? Much thought must be given to creating the symbols from decade to decade. Men in the public and humbling service of women should be a serviceable sign for a long time to come. (*Pastoral Music*, August/September 1989, page 16)

The number of participants often is much greater than 12, and in some communities the washing is extended to all present. It is common for more than one person to wash feet during the rite; one aspect of the mandatum is a kind of role reversal where the normal order of things is upset (pastor serving parishioners—which is ideally not a reversal at all), but that is not the sole image at work here. And it is common that all who wash feet also have their feet washed (pastor included). Present practice also shows an understanding that there is to be a fullness here: plenty of water (warm and sometimes with fragrant bath oil in it), real washing of the feet (both feet), drying with towels. The gesture of kissing the person's feet after washing them also is seen.

The choreography and order is important and will differ from place to place. After the homily, without anything needing to be said, the presider and others prepare to wash feet by vesting appropriately. If these ministers also are to have their feet washed, they remove their shoes and stockings at this time. Usually, the music of the mandatum begins during this preparation by the ministers.

Acolytes and helpers bring the pitchers, basins and towels and then are to assist throughout the rite. Someone is available to keep bringing warm water to refill the pitchers (necessary as this is more than a token washing).

While the ministers are preparing, those to have their feet washed take their places (although in many cases they may be seated in these places from the beginning of the liturgy). Some people might come in front of the assembly, where chairs now have been placed for them by the acolytes, but if there are steps to the area around the altar, it may be possible for people to sit on these steps and avoid moving furniture around.

The far better approach is for the washing to take place in the midst of the assembly. If the assembly sits in pews, folding chairs can be placed at the end of some pews in every aisle, scattered from front to back. In this way, the washing happens all through the assembly.

Those who wash feet work in twos or threes as needed. They settle down on their knees before each person. The one doing the washing places the large basin (which may need to be emptied after three or four washings, before it becomes too awkward to carry) under the person's feet, pours plenty of warm, fragrant water over each foot, scrubs each foot thoroughly; then, when both feet are washed, takes the towel (from the helper) to dry them. This is done without hurrying. Several "teams" of washers can be at work at the same time in all the various aisles and corners of the room. (All of these people must participate in a rehearsal, not only for the choreography but also for understanding the importance of fullness in all these gestures.)

Those who have done the washing have their own feet washed at the conclusion of the ritual. This would include the pastor and deacon. The order of this must be worked out so that it comes not as an appendage but as a natural part of the rite. Sometimes it can be done simply by having those who washed feet change places with some whose feet they washed.

No commentary is needed after the rite; all present have been part of a parable, and words will only limit what has happened. The presider and others wash their hands; the presider then vests for the eucharist and goes to the elect to dismiss them.

Music of the Mandatum

Music is one way that this rite is the deed of the whole assembly and not simply something people watch as an audience. Usually there will be music from the first preparation until the ministers are washing their hands. The sacramentary provides texts, most taken from the gospel story, but no one version of these has become well known. A hymn whose words must be followed from a page will detract from the assembly's participation in the washing itself. A responsorial piece usually is the answer, something with a refrain that is strong and thus gives a rhythm to the whole time spent in washing feet. This piece almost certainly should be one that is heard tonight and at no other time during the year. Do we have it in us to carry a small repertory of such pieces? If we find the right ones, almost certainly the answer is "yes." Two suggestions for this piece, both from *Worship,* are: "Jesus took a towel" and "Jesu, Jesu." The Taizé setting of "Mandatum novum" (GIA) is another possibility. "Jesus took a towel," by Chrysogonus Waddell, is complex enough to be interesting, short enough to be learned at once; the accompaniment can be limited to a simple tambourine throughout (letting human voices predominate as is the tradition during the first days of the Triduum). The many verses allow for a variety of cantors and choirs to take part. The words to this composition recall the story of

Jesus washing the disciples' feet, but they follow a tradition—shown in the following antiphon from the Orthodox liturgy of this day—of putting this deed of Jesus within the whole relationship of God and creation:

> The wisdom of God that restrains the untamed fury of the waters that are above the firmament, that sets a bridle on the deep and keeps back the seas, now pours water into a basin; and the Master washes the feet of the servants. The Master who wraps the heaven in clouds girds himself with a towel; and he in whose hand is the life of all things kneels down to wash the feet of the servants.

Sometimes more than one piece of music will be necessary here, but there is a caution: Music is not background, filling up the time that would otherwise be boring. Music is integral, part of what we are doing. Using several selections gives the feeling of having a tape or radio on while doing some work: Music and deed in this case have no relation to each other. If possible, a single piece of music should be the way we sing through this gesture of washing one another's feet, giving us words and a tune we will be anxious to come to each time the Triduum comes around. For those who neither wash feet nor have their feet washed, the song allows true participation in both deeds.

Misunderstandings of the Mandatum

Because so many places seem to be struggling with this rite, it may be helpful to say something about what often goes wrong. During the mid-1980s, some Chicago parishes were surveyed about their practice with the mandatum. A number of the responses offer insight into our problems.

The person conducting the study asked what was done in the parish. Pastor and staff were asked separately from some members of the assembly about the reaction to what was done. In a parish where 12 men in suits had one foot each washed by the pastor, the latter said that this "seemed the least uncomfortable way of accomplishing this ritual," that "people will accept this because it's like the 12 apostles." The reaction of a parishioner: "It was like a play."

Another parish dropped the mandatum, substituting a text where the priests rededicated themselves to priestly ministry. The parish staff said that this was done because "we want the people to know that we are committed to them, and what better time to show that than when Jesus ordained the first priests?" But the response of some who were there was: "It is a nice way to honor the priests—and it was very moving. It helps increase vocations to the priesthood."

In other parishes, the pastor and staff washed the hands of everyone present "to show how we as a staff work as a team to serve everyone." Reaction: "It was nice."

The lessons are easy: A drama is not a ritual; the former has an audience, the latter does not. Words of rededication don't belong and won't be heard. Washing hands differs from washing feet as baking potatoes differs from baking bread. Regarding the last, the appeal is that everyone can be involved, everyone can have their hands washed and even wash another's hands. As a gesture of leaving behind one time and entering another—as a person is welcomed to the church this evening—it could be strong. But here we are asked for something else, something more awkward, more embarrassing, something lengthier. It need not be done for and by all (though that is not impossible) for it to be the deed of all. It is not understood and over in one year, this washing of feet. It is complex, ambiguous and rich in meanings and it takes many years to sink in. It is argued that washing another's feet was once common and now is not in our society. But neither is laying on hands or breaking bread or sharing a common cup, yet these are far more than relics of other cultures and times. They need only be done with care and reverence to release the power of meanings.

Some still would express frustration with the washing of the feet because we should have at our disposal symbols of service that are not so easily obscured. Perhaps this is so. The caution here is that we still must deal at the liturgy with symbol. Substituting actual deeds of service is counterproductive. Ritual has to be large enough to speak over and over to Christians young and old, of all conditions, about who they are becoming. Some more obvious deed of service may be an example, but it will not be a symbol, will not be that ritual

that can rehearse us for all our living. Our problem is not that we do not have such symbols but that we have used them so badly. That poor use is seen especially in trivial gestures and wordy explanations. If our rule becomes: No explanation, full gestures, song that becomes dear to the assembly, then perhaps this unexplainable human gesture still can do its work.

Concluding the Liturgy of the Word

Before the intercessions, the elect (and catechumens and candidates) are dismissed. This often is forgotten, but not to dismiss these people is to ignore all that the dismissal has meant since they entered the catechumenate. The question arises: Dismissed to what? Isn't the whole church supposed to be here, beginning the Triduum? There are two answers. One could say that with the mandatum completed, the church has entered the Triduum and it would be appropriate for catechists to leave with the elect and candidates for some discussion of the scriptures of this night, of the mandatum itself and of the hours to come. Those catechists would not be present for the eucharistic liturgy, but that is simply not a problem this night. Like everyone, they will be there at the Vigil. But a second answer would say that on this one occasion, dispense with further instruction and just dismiss the elect and candidates to continue a quiet time of reflection and prayer at home, perhaps to return for night prayer later.

The words of dismissal to the elect should be especially focused. The presider asks the elect to stand and addresses them:

> Friends, we have entered now into the Easter Triduum, into the time when we mark our passover in Christ from death to life. Beginning tonight, we all shall join you in fasting and in vigiling, in quiet reflection and in prayer, as we approach the night of your baptism when you shall come with us to this holy table. Go now, but return to this room often in the next two days as the church keeps watch.

If there are candidates for reception into full communion with the Roman Catholic Church, they are asked to stand:

> Friends, you also will join us shortly at this table. Go now and keep the paschal fast. Return often in these days to pray.

And if there are catechumens (those who have been admitted to the catechumenate but have not been chosen for baptism at this Easter Vigil), they are asked to stand:

> Friends, this church, to which you belong as catechumens, now enters a time of prayer and fasting in expectation of Christ's death and resurrection, made real in our midst through baptism and eucharist. We await the day when you will join us at this table. Go now, but return here to pray with us often during these days.

After these people depart, the liturgy continues with the prayers of intercession (there is no creed). No special texts are provided for these. The expectation is simply that the assembly always is to intercede, to remember itself and to remind God of the afflictions and needs of the world. Certainly, the intercessions today are prepared with an awareness of the mandatum and of the collection to follow and of how these give us orientation to the world.

The rubric in the sacramentary directs: "At the beginning of the liturgy of the eucharist, there may be a procession of the faithful with gifts for the poor." The rubric, by leaving out anything about gifts for the church and by seeming to encourage a procession that is more than token, indicates that the preparation ritual today also has a once-a-year quality to it.

The Preparation of the Gifts

Parishes where various forms of lenten almsgiving have been practiced may have the tradition of bringing forward the alms at this time. Often this will be the coins and bills collected (perhaps in the "Operation Rice Bowl" boxes provided by Catholic Relief Services) day by day through Lent, especially when some fasting and simplicity in meals has been practiced. Some parishes may see this also as a time to bring clothing and other gifts for the poor, though a packed church building will not be conducive to this. The bulletin should make it clear during Lent what form of offering will be brought to the Holy Thursday liturgy and how the money (and goods) will be used. The 1988 letter of the Roman Congregation for Divine Worship spoke of this collection as "gifts for the poor, especially those collected during Lent as the fruit of penance" (#52).

The washing of the feet and this collection have much in common. That can be emphasized (without speaking of it at all) if those who washed feet and those whose feet were washed are involved in the collection. They can remain barefoot for a visible reminder of the link between the actions. These people can be the ones to pass baskets back and forth in each row. Much better on this day is the practice of simply taking the baskets into the assembly, allowing people to come into the aisles with their lenten boxes or envelopes and place these into the baskets carried by the ministers. It is something of a chaotic time, but in a longer-than-usual liturgy, that is what is needed. The filled baskets need not be placed by the altar but can be taken to a side room for safekeeping.

Bread and wine can be brought forward as this collection begins and the preparation of the table then takes place during the collection, or the collection happens first and bread and wine and money are called forward together.

The sacramentary suggests that song should be used during the procession and that the traditional "Ubi caritas" text should be considered. Many parishes use this Latin text in the Taizé setting where the assembly sings the antiphon over and over. "Where charity and love prevail" is a familiar English setting of the song.

The Eucharistic Prayer

The preface suggested in the sacramentary is Holy Eucharist I, but the following arguments could be made for alternatives. Eucharistic Prayer II, with its own preface, would give a greater simplicity to this liturgy. The first Eucharistic Prayer for Masses of Reconciliation, with its own preface, has a sense of the paschal mystery and a concern for unity. Two prefaces should be considered when deciding about this day's liturgy: Sacred Heart (P45) and Holy Cross (P46); the latter is the basic text of the preface for Passiontide in the calendar before 1970. Both of these texts address the larger context of the Triduum.

Good Sunday habits for the eucharistic prayer regarding gesture, posture, speech, acclamations and pace will largely determine today's prayer. As noted earlier, the eucharistic liturgy today is best kept simple and direct. Note that there are inserts for Eucharistic Prayer I; this prayer is not required, but may be a good choice.

When additional priests concelebrate this liturgy, the manner of doing so is to be determined and communicated well beforehand. Concelebrants need not stand at the table; in the few times when they speak, the assembly is to hear the principal celebrant's voice clearly (*General Instruction*, #170). No texts need be assigned for any of the concelebrants to speak alone; the usual experience is that using several speakers does not support a sense of unity at the eucharistic table.

If there is a deacon, the deacon and not a concelebrant assists the presider at the altar. If there is no deacon, there is no need for anyone to assist the presider. Regarding the presence of a deacon at this liturgy: Only if the deacon regularly assists with the principal Sunday eucharist should there be a deacon at this liturgy. The deacon then should be part of all rehearsals for the liturgy.

The acclamations of the eucharistic prayer could be those used during Lent, especially if these are to be used also in Eastertime as a sign of the unity of the whole paschal season. In general, the eucharistic prayer is done with all the strength that the parish has developed for its Sunday liturgy; no flourishes need be added.

The Communion Rite

Again, the good Sunday practice of the parish suffices for tonight. The Lord's Prayer is recited or sung, the sign of peace is exchanged and the bread is broken. No extra texts or commentary is needed. Because every Sunday liturgy should include large loaves of bread (see the recipe in the appendix, part 7), there is nothing different tonight except this: Enough bread must be present and broken for the communion tomorrow. Cups and plates are brought to the altar, as usual, only after the peace greeting when the presider has begun the breaking of the bread. The ministers of communion break and distribute the bread into plates and pour the wine into cups. The Lamb of God is sung as usual all through this time. A good practice is for the communion ministers to go to their stations as soon as they receive their plate or cup; they then turn toward the altar until the assembly has recited, "Lord, I am not worthy." They receive communion themselves after the rest of the assembly.

The communion song, with a refrain that is taken up fully by the assembly, should begin immediately after the invitation to the table and should last until all have received.

This liturgy is not an appropriate time for first communion. The liturgies of the Vigil, of Easter Day and of the whole Eastertime are appropriate.

After communion, the ministers take the plates and cups to the credence table; they receive communion and consume any wine that remains. No wine is reserved. All the vessels are covered, to be purified later. The remaining bread is placed in one vessel and this is taken to the altar. Nothing else remains on the altar.

The *Circular Letter* suggests the following:

> It is most opportune that at the time of communion deacons, acolytes, or special ministers receive the eucharist from the table of the altar to bring it afterwards to the sick, so that they may receive communion at home and in this way be able to share more closely in the Church's celebration.

Perhaps the hour of the night will suggest a different practice: that the sick and infirm be visited on Friday and Saturday, not with communion but with prayers that manifest their unity to the church as that church continues to assemble through the Triduum. The time for sharing in the holy communion, then, ideally would be on Sunday morning, with ministers coming directly from the parish eucharist.

When the communion of the assembly and ministers is completed, the presider and the whole assembly now are seated for some time of silence or for the singing of a psalm or song of praise. After this, all stand and the presider (remaining at the chair) recites the prayer after communion from the sacramentary.

The Procession

If the catechesis and the practice of other years has been good, then nothing at all need be said to the assembly about what now takes place. If something is said, it should be direct and brief:

> Sisters and brothers, we have begun the Paschal Triduum. From now until the Vigil on Saturday night, the whole church is fasting, praying and

keeping watch. Some of us will go now to the tabernacle with the body of Christ that is communion for the sick, viaticum for the dying and our food at the liturgy of Good Friday. Many may wish to join this procession; all are welcome to stay here in prayer or to return later, especially for night prayer. When you take leave, please do so in a spirit of quiet.

In any case, this is not a solemn procession but a simple action of taking the bread to the tabernacle. The sacramentary says that this is a "transfer," not benediction or any other ritual. This rite is without words except for those of the song sung by the assembly. The sense here is for the presence of Jesus with us, with the church, in these days. The beautiful hymn that the assembly sings, perhaps in Latin and in English and in other languages of the parish, is the "Pange Lingua," written by Thomas Aquinas. This text is acclamation of the passover, the passing over of Jesus and of the church. It is acclamation of our encounter with that passover, food and drink for us, body and blood for us.

The presider goes to the altar, places incense in the thurible, kneels and honors the reserved sacrament with the incense. Then the presider receives the humeral veil and takes the vessel (if more than one, a deacon or another minister should carry any additional vessels); the song and the procession begin. The cross (but see the previous discussion about the place of the cross and the Good Friday liturgy), candles and incense precede the presider; the assembly follows. If the procession goes outside, where it is difficult to maintain song, members of the choir should be stationed at key places to keep the singing strong. If the procession moves to a small room within the same building, only a few ministers and a few members of the assembly can join the procession. Those that remain can continue singing through the verses of the hymn. This allows the liturgy to "fade out," rather than to end. Some will leave at once, but many probably will stay to pray silently. Some of the ministers can return in a few moments to also sit here and there in the room and pray.

Where there is a full procession, the singing continues until all who have joined the procession are at the chapel where the tabernacle is placed. The presider again puts incense in the thurible and again honors the reserved sacrament with incense. The tabernacle then is closed and the hymn concludes.

The rubrics clearly indicate that the procession moves to a "chapel." The sense is another room altogether from the church (which is the same sense the postconciliar documents have for the location of the tabernacle: in a space apart from the place where the eucharist is celebrated). The rubrics (and #49 in the *Circular Letter*) clearly indicate that the parish's tabernacle is to be in this chapel only if the chapel is a space clearly separated from the main worship space. If it is not, if the tabernacle still is located in the main worship space, then the parish should create a temporary chapel in which a tabernacle will be placed. This tabernacle could be a suitable but temporary receptacle. It is clear from the rubrics that any tabernacle in the main worship space is to remain empty from before this night's liturgy at least until the end of the Vigil.

Neither in the church nor in this place is there a blessing or dismissal. The church is now in the Triduum. Some ministers may take leave; others may remain in prayer. The same is true of the assembly. Sometimes the sense of silence actually is enhanced if, during this time when some are leaving, the choir begins and many join in a quiet refrain (such as the Taizé compositions "Stay with me" or "Jesus, remember me"). The rubrics direct that prayer in this place not continue after midnight.

Prayer in the church itself, however, is appropriate throughout the night and all the hours of the Triduum. The sense should be that the great hall of this church is open and is where anyone can come at any time to renew their sense for the watching and praying of these days. No group should organize its prayer during this time in such a way that anyone from the parish would feel excluded.

In the church itself, anything not carried out in procession now is removed (e.g., the altar cloth, the vessels used in tonight's liturgy). This is done quietly and in the spirit of prayer that now fills the church. The tradition of reciting Psalm 22 at this time could be retained. This is the type of simple insight that makes all the practical gestures of these days into part of the Triduum itself.

The Paschal Fast: Keeping the Time before the Vigil

Later we will consider the various rites that must or may take place from late on Thursday night until the beginning of the Vigil on Saturday night. Here we look at something more basic: the wholeness of this time and its observance.

Both those who regularly bring themselves to the assembly and those who rarely come should notice these days being kept hour by hour and minute by minute in the lives of pastor, staff, parishioners.

At some times and in some places during our first centuries, this Sunday near Passover became a time for baptisms: The stories told of Israel's passing over from slavery to freedom and of Jesus' passing over, his baptism of passion and death and resurrection, surrounded the present deed of the church. New Christians passed over from old ways to new ways, sometimes from ways of slavery and death to life and freedom. Because that action was not taken lightly, because Christians knew what most tribes set on initiating new members know, there was a time of preparation. The preparation was a discipline that included but went beyond fasting from food and drink.

That initiation and its immediate and intense preparation are the origins of our Triduum. Time passed. Ways of initiation changed. The days before Easter came to be associated with the various moments in the passion, death and resurrection of Christ. Various observances evolved. The Vigil liturgy, celebrated on a Saturday morning, seldom was part of the experience of most Catholics. Lent, as a time of penance, ended on noon on Holy Saturday. The next day was Easter Sunday; in its liturgy, it was not much different from any other Sunday of the year. Through these times, Holy Thursday and Good Friday and even Easter itself (more among some ethnic groups than others) were holy days for many Catholics and they were kept with many devotions and customs, though without recognizable connections to initiation.

Restoring the Paschal Fast

The reform of the calendar for Holy Week began during the 1950s. It restored appropriate times and removed inappropriate elements from the liturgies of these days. The reform of the whole calendar at the end of the 1960s, following Vatican II, carried this further with its definitions of Lent and Eastertime. Two other movements have been instrumental in giving us our present Triduum. First is the restoration of initiation of adults as an order by which the local church receives inquirers, nourishes catechumens and calls them eventually to prepare for baptism at the Vigil. Second (and the business of this chapter) is the dawning sense that seasons and feasts are not only their liturgies but must be "rites" of their own.

Lent and Fridays had given Catholics some sense for what "keeping" time means, but this was not always positive because of so much legalism and so many loopholes. Even so, these penitential days gave some notion of identity: Being Catholic required public disciplines, like not eating meat, like fasting. Our concern here is not so much the public character of this (how such things come across in the marketplace), but simply that they require that I identify myself to myself as belonging to this people who do such and such because our calendar says it is that time. The work that such a ritual of time does goes far beyond building this sense of identity: For better or worse, it forms me in the ways of this people; in the now familiar expression, it forms in me the habits of the heart.

The *Constitution on the Sacred Liturgy*, ratified in 1963 by the bishops of the world at Vatican II, contains ten paragraphs on the liturgical year. These call for major reforms of the calendar. Lent is the only season dealt with: Its "baptismal and penitential aspects" are to be given greater prominence "in both the liturgy and liturgical catechesis." The Triduum as such never is mentioned in the *Constitution*, but the last two sentences of the paragraphs on Lent mark a startling new beginning:

> Let the paschal fast be kept sacred. Let it be observed everywhere on Good Friday and, where possible, prolonged through Holy Saturday, as a way of coming to the joys of the Sunday of the resurrection with uplifted and welcoming heart.

Except for some shifting of regulations about fast and abstinence, this was not noticed much at first. But it is a remarkable call for reform.

What is a *paschal* fast? What makes it different from any other fast? What does it mean to keep such a fast "sacred"? What type of fasting is being called for? What kind of fasting over two days is capable of creating an "uplifted and welcoming heart"? Nearly 30 years after the Council, the questions have yet to be widely asked.

This summons to the paschal fast has been echoed in various documents since the Council. The *General Norms for the Liturgical Year and the Calendar* in 1969 identified the Easter Triduum as a time distinct from Lent and Eastertime and said this:

> On Good Friday and, if possible, also on Holy Saturday until the Easter Vigil, the Easter fast is observed everywhere. (#20)

In the *Rite of Christian Initiation of Adults* (1972, adapted for use in the United States, 1988) the rubrics speak of the immediate preparation of the elect:

> The elect are to be advised that on Holy Saturday they should refrain from their usual activities, spend their time in prayer and reflection, and, as far as they can, observe a fast. (#185)

In 1988, the *Circular Letter* repeated and emphasized the original call of the *Constitution on the Sacred Liturgy*:

> The fast on the first two days of the Triduum is especially sacred: according to an early tradition the Church fasts because these are the days when "Christ its Spouse was taken away." On Good Friday the fast must be observed along with abstinence and it is recommended that this

fast be continued on Holy Saturday, so that the Church may come to the joys of Easter Sunday in joy and exaltation. (#39)

When this document speaks of "ancient tradition," it has in mind the third-century *Apostolic Tradition;* in that description of early church life, we are told that "those who are to receive baptism shall fast on the Preparation (Friday) and on the Sabbath (Saturday)."

Discovering the Church Fasting

Why has this summons by various documents over 30 years made so little impact? Why do so many still think of Good Friday, a day of fasting and abstinence, exactly as they think of Ash Wednesday?

Perhaps for many of us the answer is the culture, the times. We do not imagine deeds that need this type of preparation. It may very well occur to us to skip some meals as a penitential or an intercessory gesture, but we don't intuitively feel that one cannot rise from the table after a grand meal and go to the Easter Vigil. We have not yet come, as a church, to such excitement and awe for what takes place in the darkness between Saturday and Sunday that we have no appetite anyway. Yet, if we trust the *Constitution on the Sacred Liturgy,* it works the other way around. That is, it is the fasting itself that will bring us to the Vigil with a heart and a mind that can know awe and excitement.

That is the significance of a "paschal" fast, and that is the importance of helping people understand that we fast in different ways for different reasons. The fasting of Lent is penitential. It begins on Ash Wednesday and it ends the afternoon of Holy Thursday. It is no liturgical fine point that Good Friday and its fast are not even in Lent. There is a turning, as we enter the Triduum on Thursday, when we let ourselves focus fully on what is to be at the Vigil. With that, the fasting of Friday and Saturday is not penitential but anticipatory. It is a fasting that comes from the same part of us that has us fast before momentous events in our lives. Few are hungry on the morning of their wedding day. This is that type of fast.

> There is a time in every human life when we turn from food because we are so filled with something else. Perhaps we are in mourning, or in love, or writing an article, or painting a picture, or reading a wonderful novel. We fast because we are no longer hungry, but are utterly filled with

something else. The paschal fast is being so filled with God that nothing else counts, and other things could only distract. (James Field, "The Paschal Fast," *Assembly,* March 1980)

Such fasting is not only from food. Even more important may be the fasting from our normal work, the fasting from seeking ways to be entertained, the fasting from much chatter, the stilling of our cultural hunger for diversion. Catholics are called to live these days unlike any other of the year—and this is so whatever economic condition we are in, whatever our work, whatever our family situation, whatever our educational background. It is a great leveler, like the eucharist itself, this paschal fast.

These are years to explore the ways a church keeps this fast. We need not fall into dozens of regulations and more dozens of loopholes. But we do need the practical examples, and we need each other. This can't be done all alone. It is the church that is fasting. Strong example has to come from those in leadership. Business as usual in the rectory kitchen means the Triduum has not been received there. Those who lead have to explore among themselves what this Triduum and its fasting look like and why. The conversation goes from year to year as does the effort at catechesis and the building up of solid liturgical practice. The church, the baptized and the elect, has to discover why these days must be different if there is to be any reality, any truth, to what we do at the Vigil.

Here, finally, is what it means that our liturgy is not magic, is not there at the snap of our fingers. For a people to do their liturgy, they must have done something else. For a people to do the vigiling and the renouncing and the promising and the baptizing and the eucharist, they must come hungry, famished, for God's word, for the deeds they do in community, for the water and for the bread and the wine.

The Fast and the Liturgy

The documents previously quoted speak of coming to our Easter with an "uplifted and welcoming heart." They say that the paschal fast is meant to give us that kind of heart. "Lift up your hearts," we hear every Sunday: *Sursum corda,* the Latin said. That is the notion here: an uplifted heart. The fast is to be such that after Friday and Saturday—without much food, without much distraction of any kind—we will have our hearts set right. The assembly on Saturday night, then, is a hungry crowd, starving almost, ready to devour word and sacrament. Fasting clarifies, puts in perspective, sharpens—just as it can irritate and preoccupy, especially the novice (one has to practice, make it a good habit).

When the church is fasting—and that always should be understood here as multifaceted—then the whole person is making ready for the Vigil. The destination, as is so often the lesson we learn, doesn't happen without the journey. This destination is a work of that whole person. Mind and heart and body and imagination and passion are all involved in a church's Easter. Those who thus prepare are going to come to the Vigil knowing that if this is going to get done, they are the ones who have to do it. It isn't done for them or to them but is the work of the whole hungry assembly.

A parish awareness of this discipline won't come about in a year and it won't come about around this one occasion. It will depend on an ongoing awareness that the church keeps a rhythm of fasting in its life. Having had a generation or so without much awareness of this, it perhaps is time for us to discover it again. Besides the fasting of these days, there is the lenten fast that went before. We also have, in the United States, the strong invitation from our bishops to return to the practice of a fast on Fridays, to do penance in the cause of justice and of peace. And we have some small movement toward a rediscovery of the seasonal penance once embodied in ember days (see *Catholic Household Blessings and Prayers*). These last expand the penitential side of fasting.

The fast before celebrating the eucharist, now just one hour, shows another expression of the anticipatory fasting that we are doing on Good Friday and Holy Saturday. These are two facets of our Catholic way of fasting; both are meant to go beyond the fast from food. Both have the potential, like so much in our lives, to free or enslave, to wake us up or put us to sleep, to open or to close:

> What then is fasting for us Christians? It is our entrance and participation in that experience of Christ himself by which he liberates us from the total dependence on food, matter, and the world. By no means is our liberation a full one. Living still in the fallen world, in the world of the Old Adam, being part of it, we still depend on food. But just as our

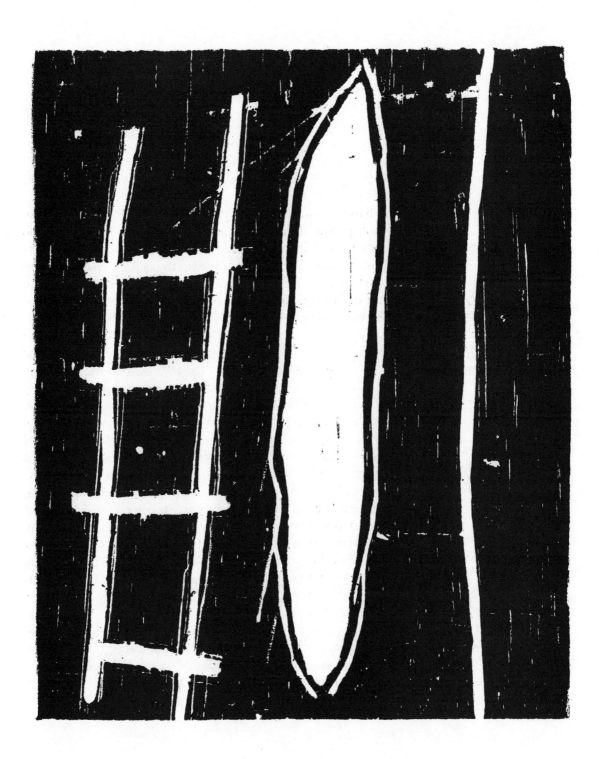

death—through which we still must pass—has become by virtue of Christ's death a passage into life, the food we eat and the life it sustains can be in this life and in this world that which strengthens us, our communion with God, rather than that which separates us from God. Yet it is only fasting that can perform that transformation, giving us the existential proof that our dependence on food and matter are not total, not absolute, that united to prayer, grace and adoration, it can itself be spiritual. (Alexander Schmemann, *Great Lent,* St. Vladimir's Seminary Press, page 96)

These powerful insights from a theologian of the Russian Orthodox church remind us that in East and West fasting is to be something positive. It is a way to paradise, to the garden where we will undo that original eating from a tree. Our fasting readies us for the messianic time whose strongest image, in any tribe, is the great banquet. We want to be very hungry.

Parish Practice

Some of the notions discussed previously may be helpful, in homily or bulletin, in presenting anew the notion of the paschal fast. Two things probably are necessary, besides example and patience.

First, especially where there are to be baptisms at the Vigil and so the parish has had a long and important and conscious relationship with the catechumens/elect, the fast is to be presented as something that makes us ready to baptize. Our fast is that of the whole church, the baptized standing beside the elect as they enter the final struggle to receive baptism into the death of Jesus. This means that the whole process of initiation as it is undertaken year after year is a central and serious task that to some extent involves everyone. That should hardly need saying, but our culture intimidates: It is hard for us to take baptism for what we say it is. We would rather be somewhat light about it: So glad to have you in the club. Even immersion in the waters can be fun, like an initiation into a fraternity or sorority rather than death to oneself and life in Christ. This is exactly where the presence of the catechumens and elect and newly baptized is to reform the church. The summons to fast, the need to fast, as we approach the font will prove and strengthen this reformation.

Second, the invitation to the fast will be heard in some close proportion to the strength of the Easter Vigil liturgy as it is celebrated year after year. It is difficult to imagine the motivation for the paschal fast if a person either does not attend the Vigil or experiences the Vigil, poorly done, as something without meaning or power. This fast goes somewhere, it gets us to the Vigil's marvelous scriptures, to its alleluia, to the font and the chrism and the table. Being there one year, we are a little more ready to embrace the fast the next time around.

In presenting the invitation to the paschal fast, the unity of Friday and Saturday is stressed, in part by pointing out that Saturday is the more logical day than Friday for fasting, as it leads directly to the Vigil. Friday is fitting because it is 1) the day when our celebration of the paschal mystery focuses on the death and burial of our Lord, 2) the day before this Saturday and its Vigil, 3) a Friday, which in itself invites fasting (the day the bridegroom is taken away) and 4) long a day of the legal fast and abstinence.

In its invitation, the parish can present the church's norm for fast and abstinence. But clearly the *Constitution on the Sacred Liturgy* and the other documents are talking about a fast that goes beyond the "one full meal a day" notion. One full meal a day probably will not get us to that "uplifted and welcoming heart." Sometimes, the parish commitment to plain, shared meals on Friday and Saturday evenings will help some engage in keeping these two days. Bread and soup should do, resisting all the natural urges to put more things on the table.

The invitation should stress that food and drink are not the whole of the fast, or perhaps even most important. In our day, it is surely as important that the television and radio and other entertainment devices are turned off. Our hunger for distracting ourselves is huge; we get the message over and over that we need this diversion and that diversion. These are not days to catch up on exercise or for reading the stack of magazines or whatever else is tempting.

The tradition, still known in some places today, is to fast also from work, from one's livelihood, from earning money and spending money. If that only frees us for other work, it probably is wasted.

These days are about struggle, but in a strange way they also are about rest, freedom from work.

Watch and Pray

It is within the fast that the faithful gather to pray. Throughout Friday and Saturday, there are many moments of common prayer in the parish church. All of them are words and gestures about how the Lord's passover more and more defines our own lives. There is the sense that the church, once gathered on Thursday night, does not disperse. Some people are always there as they take turns vigiling and the number swells a bit for morning prayer, for the three hours of Friday, for the simple rites with the elect during the day on Saturday. Many more come for the more solemn rituals of Good Friday. The house of the church, that place where we normally gather each Sunday for eucharist, truly begins to be a house of the church during these days, a place that's lived in by those who watch and pray.

Some parishes have sign-up sheets so that individuals and organizations can fill in all the hours of day and night in the church. The parish can provide scripture and books of prayer for those who come. The continuous reading aloud of the gospels is possible, along with selections from the Hebrew Scriptures, prepared in a loose-leaf book that could be handed from one person to another, with good times of silence. A number of cards with appropriate psalms on them also could be available, allowing people to pray psalms together. (*A Triduum Sourcebook,* available from Liturgy Training Publications, would be a suitable prayer book for these days in many parishes.)

Good Friday: The Celebration of the Lord's Passion

Of Good Friday, the *Circular Letter* says:

> On this day "when Christ became our paschal sacrifice," the church reflects on the Passion of its Lord and Spouse, adores his cross, commemorates its own origin from the side of the dead Christ on the cross, and intercedes for the salvation of the entire world. (#58)

This is not only a description of the afternoon liturgy of this day, but of the day itself. Each of the actions mentioned (reflects, adores, commemorates, intercedes) is worthy of reflection early in the process of preparing both the whole Triduum and this day's central liturgy.

The sacramentary names that liturgy of Good Friday the Celebration of the Lord's Passion. The rubrics stress that there is to be but one celebration of this liturgy in each community, though in the United States the bishop may allow the liturgy to be repeated "if the size or nature of the parish" so indicates. The language here is less strict than that of the Thursday night liturgy and much less strict than that of the Vigil. The language would perhaps admit a second celebration in another language if that were desirable, but with the permission of the bishop. Likewise, a repetition of this liturgy might be called for because of large numbers, but there is no hint of multiplying the liturgy for the sake of convenience.

The sacramentary's rubric regarding the time for this liturgy reads: "The celebration of the Lord's passion takes place in the afternoon, about three o'clock, unless pastoral reasons suggest a later hour." The *Circular Letter* of 1988 expands on this:

> Celebration of the Lord's Passion should take place in the afternoon, at around three o'clock (15:00). But pastoral considerations will suggest

the most opportune time, that is, an hour when the people may most easily gather, for example, some time after noon or later in the evening, but not after nine o'clock. (#63)

What is clear is the central place of this liturgy. The parish first would determine its time, then go on to arrange the hours of Morning and Evening Prayer, perhaps stations of the cross (if this is the tradition) and other times for scheduled prayers.

The Room

The appearance of the church (that is, the house of the church) is something like our appearance: fasting, without distractions. All the clutter (from the whole room and the entryways, not just the area around the altar) was removed at the beginning of Lent. Most of the decoration was taken away before yesterday's liturgy. It is a hall with a table and an empty font and a reading stand and some places for people to sit. Some of the directives suggest that any crosses be removed (though at places where the image has been multiplied, this probably is unwise). The holy water fonts are removed or sealed.

Few things are needed for this liturgy and they are not present when it begins. Only the sacramentary (or specially prepared presider's book) is required from the beginning. A lector should have the lectionary.

The presider and deacon wear red vestments, as at Mass. Any other priests and deacons are not vested and take places in the assembly.

Overview

The liturgy begins with silent and spoken prayer, followed by the liturgy of the word. This is the usual structure of scripture, silence, psalmody, scripture, silence, gospel acclamation, the proclamation of the passion, homily, intercessions. The intercessions are in an elaborate form. The cross is then carried solemnly into the assembly (or, if already present, is solemnly presented) and is venerated by all. The rite concludes with the simplest of communion services and the liturgy ends, as it began, in silence.

This liturgy makes no effort toward including an entrance rite or a concluding rite. There is no need for this: This church assembled last night, entered into the Triduum and remains there. Various members have come at different times to pray, and the prayer goes on in homes and other places and here in the church. Those who prepare this liturgy are to avoid any effort to change this. The liturgy should begin as if simply resuming in a public way what has gone on in private ways. It should end in such a way that one can hardly be sure it has ended—because it hasn't.

If there is a problem in preparing this liturgy, it is that there are too many high points and too few low. The first two readings are strong texts; the passion demands attention; the intercessions are in a once-a-year form and must be unhurried; the veneration of the cross has the music and movement that make it the logical high point of the liturgy. Only the communion service is without emphasis.

The preparation then must be involved with the pace, with what each element seems to demand and with all that involves going from here to there (in time as well as in the space). For example, in the intercessions, careful preparation will entail thinking about the texts to be used; about the rehearsal of the ministers and how speaking (or chanting) the call to prayer differs from speaking (or chanting) the prayer itself; about the length of the pause between the two spoken (or chanted) parts; about the use of any spoken or sung refrain at some point in each prayer; about the location of the leaders and the posture of the assembly; about the transition from the homily to these intercessions and from the intercessions to the veneration of the cross.

Those preparing should assume that people want to be here and that the length of the liturgy is independent of Sunday morning expectations. That simply frees the liturgy to have its proper pace; it does not say what the length is going to be. We deal with all those "high points" by giving ourselves some space, some room in the pace of this liturgy to reflect and regather.

Preparation also involves a sense for the tone of this liturgy. That is gleaned from the texts, from the place of this liturgy within the whole of the Triduum and from experience. It is this tone that is communicated to the ministers in the rehearsals. Words such as *somber, reflective* and *in no hurry* may provide some of this. We also need notions of being at home and at ease in these structures of scripture reading, song and prayer. But in addition to all this, the tone of the liturgy has to do with its place in the Triduum itself.

Here it plays a number of roles. It is about sorrow. It is about all our grief. It is about the glory we proclaim in the cross. It is about that which we proclaim to ourselves, the elect and the world: the folly, foolishness and stumbling block that is the cross—"May I never boast of anything except the cross of our Lord Jesus Christ, by which the world has been crucified to me, and I to the world." Liturgy is always multifaceted, always holding contradictions tightly together and daring us to apply our logic. Today's liturgy knows that well and it should be presented for reflection to all who minister.

There is nothing in today's liturgy that requires the presider to be an ordained priest or deacon. The United States Bishops' Committee on the Liturgy, however, in responding to various questions, has said that when a priest is present in the community, that priest should preside. If there is a deacon but no priest, the deacon should preside.

This liturgy has no provision for anything that resembles concelebration. All clergy who work or reside in the parish and any deacons other than the one assigned to this liturgy, even though they have no ministerial role, should be present in the assembly. This is true of all the liturgies of the Triduum, for it makes no sense to insist that these are for the whole parish and to encourage everyone to be present, then to have any ordained persons absent. The same could well be said for all members of the parish staff and for all parishioners who take leadership roles on the parish council or in other ways.

Instruments normally would be used only to support singing; some would argue that if the singing can be done well without that support, this should be done (another application of our fasting during these days).

Beginning

Any preparation for the liturgy should be completed at least half an hour early so that there is silence and stillness in the room as people assemble. The liturgy may begin with a silent procession of the ministers, but there is no need for this. At least 20 to 30 minutes before the time scheduled for this liturgy, the presider (and deacon) and the acolytes, without any procession, take places near the altar, sitting with the assembly. At the proper time, they rise and stand in place until the whole assembly joins them in standing. Then they move to a position between the assembly and the altar. They bow deeply and reverently to the altar, then they kneel down.

They should remain in a kneeling posture until the whole assembly has knelt. No signal is necessary, but it helps if some persons in the front know that the assembly is to kneel at this point. Even in churches where there are no kneelers attached to the chairs or benches, this is a time when all are to go on their knees.

When all are kneeling and the noise has ceased, the ministers prostrate themselves. The rubric in the sacramentary makes this optional, but the *Circular Letter* is quite firm:

> The procession of the priest and ministers to the altar takes place in silence, without singing. Any introductory comments are to be made before the entrance of the ministers.
>
> After a reverence to the altar, the priest and ministers prostrate themselves. As a rite peculiar to this day, this prostration is to be sedulously retained as a sign of both "our earthly nature" and of the mourning and grief of the Church.
>
> The faithful stand during the entrance of the ministers, and then kneel in silent prayer. (#65)

It would be fully appropriate for the whole assembly to take on this same posture should the room and furniture allow.

The prostration should last well beyond the time when the room quiets down. It is a once-a-year ritual, but even so there will be a memory from year to year, and the assembly should know that there will be a long time—two or three minutes at least—to pray silently.

At the end of this time, the presider rises and goes to the chair. If necessary, the presider can gesture for all to stand. An acolyte holds the book. There is no greeting, no introduction, no invitation to pray, no extra words of any kind. When all are standing and quiet, the presider sings or recites the prayer. Neither of the two texts provided in the sacramentary is especially strong in the present version; the second is perhaps better, but "Adam" should be "Adam and Eve" and "his manhood" certainly means "their humanity." The collect that is used throughout the liturgy of the hours today has a great simplicity to it; the petition part, usually a long element in a collect, is only "behold." In its *Book of Common Prayer* version, it also uses inclusive language:

> Almighty God, we pray you graciously to behold this your family, for whom our Lord Jesus Christ was willing to be betrayed, and given into the hands of sinners, and to suffer death upon the cross; who now lives and reigns with you and the Holy Spirit, one God, for ever and ever.

After the Amen, the presider and all are seated and attend to the reader.

The First Readings

In parishes where it is the regular practice to dismiss young children on Sundays for their own celebration of the liturgy of the word, this also could be done today. They would go to a separate place until the veneration of the cross. The decision to divide the assembly during any of these liturgies of the Triduum should not be made lightly. On Thursday, it never should be necessary (who would want to miss the mandatum?), and the presumption is that very young children are not present at the Vigil. But today the liturgy of the word, including the intercessions, is lengthy. If the children have their own liturgy of the word, it must be that: a liturgy. Those who preside should take care that it does not become a class, much less a day-care program. The scriptures are to be heard and talked about; songs are to be sung. The intercessions today are especially important to the church and also should form a vital part of the children's liturgy. If this is done, the children would be called forward before the first reading and sent out in silence with their presiders. They can return before the veneration of the cross, perhaps even in the procession with the cross.

The liturgy of the word has the same structure as every Sunday's liturgy. The lectionary can be in place before the liturgy begins or the lector can bring it to the ambo. The first reading, Isaiah 52:13—53:12, establishes the tone of this gathering more powerfully than any commentary. The reader must be someone who has shown that she or he knows how to do the hard work of bringing such a text to the assembly. In most places, special participation aids will have been printed for these days and people will not have the scripture texts in their hands. If this is a new situation for the parish, all the more reason for the lector to be a vehicle for the powerful and amazing images of this long text. The pace will be varied with the nature of the passage itself, but never so quick that words and images are lost.

As for the text from Isaiah, it is clear why followers of Jesus find meaning and understanding here. It should be equally clear that there is something here that goes far beyond a reflection on the passion and death of Jesus. These are words about the experience of Israel centuries before Jesus, and they are words about how these two peoples, Jews and Christians, understand sin and redemption.

As on Sundays, the silence after the reading should be long enough for quiet to come and for reflection.

The psalm is the first singing by the assembly and cantor. Psalm 31 is assigned, with the refrain, "Father, I put my life in your hands." Psalm 22, which the parish used on Passion Sunday, is the seasonal psalm for this time (see the lectionary, #175) and so can be substituted for Psalm 31. The refrain assigned to Psalm 22 is "My God, my God, why have you abandoned me?" Accompaniment should be minimal or none at all.

The second reading is quieter and more straightforward in presentation than the first, but it builds toward the lines that need to be heard well: "Christ offered prayers and supplication with loud cries and tears to God, who was able to save him from death, and he was heard because of his reverence."

Follow this reading also with ample silence.

The proclamation of the gospel today may begin with the acclamation used throughout Lent and its own proper verse. The assembly would stand to sing this acclamation. There is, however, no provision in today's liturgy for carrying in a book of gospels at the beginning of the liturgy and placing it on the altar. If there is a single reader of the passion, the reading is taken from the lectionary already in place. There is no procession of book, candles and

The Passion Reading

incense. Candles and incense are not used in this liturgy until the veneration of the cross. There also is no greeting and no signing of the book or the person at the beginning of the reading. The gospel does, however, conclude in the usual way: "The gospel of the Lord." "Praise to you, Lord Jesus Christ."

In an ideal situation, all would stand as usual for the gospel. But in many places, it now is customary because of the length of the passion reading to invite all to be seated. Sitting or standing should not be left to the individual: Dividing the assembly is unwise. If any invitation is given (and the presumption should be that Catholics stand as the gospel is read), it should be for all. Rather than a spoken instruction, some persons in the front could know that after the announcement ("The Passion of our Lord Jesus Christ according to John") they are to sit down. The reader waits until all are then seated and attentive. If this is done, then at a certain place, after the words "Pilate handed Jesus over to be crucified," the reader pauses and (led by those in the front who have been rehearsed) all stand. After the words, "and delivered over his spirit," all, including the reader, may kneel in silence for at least a full minute (if anything less, there never is any real silence in most assemblies).

Many parishes continue the acclamation of the gospel, as it were, with song verses interspersed through the text. This gives a reflective pace to the reading and helps all to hear what is being read. The words of any hymn would be in the participation aid, with clear indications of when each is to be sung. The choice of verses for singing should be dictated by the liturgy and by John's unique telling of this story. The model for this choice might be the "Vexilla Regis" hymn, "The royal banners forward go" in its own tune or with another tune that fits the meter and the spirit of this hymn. Another translation of this hymn, using a different meter (CM), is found in *Hymnal for the Hours* (GIA): "The regal dark mysterious cross." "Sing, my tongue, the song of triumph," also suggested for the entrance on Holy Thursday, would be appropriate. These two ancient hymns share the theology of John's gospel: The cross is our glory. Similar verses are found in "O cross of Christ, immortal tree," also in *Hymnal for the Hours* (GIA). In any of these, the disadvantage is that the assembly must hold and watch the participation aid. This can be avoided by choosing a Taizé or other ostinato or a reflective refrain for these reflective acclamations of the passion reading.

The manner in which the passion is recited or sung also needs attention. Any approach that has the assembly read the parts of the crowd should be avoided. If there is a missalette in use in the parish and it calls for this, consider removing it from the pews for today's liturgy. If this is not possible, then there should be a direct, simple invitation before the reader begins the passion: "You are asked to put aside the missalette and to listen with all attention to the reading of the passion."

This practice of using reflective and acclamatory song within the reading of the passion was discussed by Andrew Ciferni in the January 1992 *Liturgy 90*. Ciferni argues that the use of a single reader and of assembly song at specified moments within the reading is pastoral and in line with the best of the tradition. He suggests that the places chosen for song be in accord with the gospel author's own divisions of the story. He adds:

> [This approach] carries greater respect both for the gospel text itself and for the nature of ritual proclamation. It introduces a response at critical junctures in the text itself rather than as interruptions within the various sections of the text. Thus the assembly's song works in a way similar to other responses to the word within the liturgy. Of equal importance is the preservation of the dialogic nature of worship, i.e., the assembly attends to the proclamation itself rather than to the text. Finally, the assembly's text is an authentic song of praise and/or intercession integral to worship rather than a shout more suitable to a passion play.

Should there be one reader, three readers, many readers? Should the passion be chanted or read? The passion can be chanted in the traditional tone by three singers (an English version is available from GIA Publications); the presider need not be one of the singers. But even this leans toward the dramatic, toward the passion play, when what we want is confrontation with the mystery in these well-known words. The church is not so much to be impressed or awed or moved by these words; the church is to be transformed. Where a parish has some tradition of using a passion-play approach to the reading today, it can first be suggested that this be done at some time apart from the liturgy and, if possible, apart from the Triduum. This is difficult for people who have invested much time and energy and have been rewarded with many compliments, but there are reasons to offer apart from the one argued here (that this type of dramatization betrays the nature of ritual). For example, it can be argued that the dramatic nature of the passion play overpowers the veneration of the cross, which should be the climax of the day's liturgy.

The best course usually will be a single reader who is able to proclaim the story with great strength. Such a reading presumes that the story and its phrases are well known to the assembly and builds on that. This reader presumes that these words are foundational words for us that need attention so that they may year after year take us further into the mystery that they proclaim, our own mystery.

The gospel read on Good Friday does not vary with the three years of the cycle. It is always the passion according to John. John's gospel is read by the church a good deal toward the end of Lent and this reading continues on many Sundays and weekdays of Eastertime. The reading this day centers all this other reading. From early on, the church recognized in John the text it needed to unfold around its celebration of the Passover.

That John's passion account is read on Good Friday testifies to our understanding of the Triduum's unity: John does not tell a story that would leave us mourning—trembling certainly, but not mourning. This gospel understands that the suffering and crucifixion and burial are the Pasch: the love of God catching hold of our world. To be lifted up on the cross is to be glorified. This is the Pasch, the revelation of God's love and glory. John tells a story about the meaning of what happened, and that is dear to us in these days.

But there is a great problem for us with John's passion narrative. That is the anti-Jewish character of the language and of the tone. John's account uses the word "Jews" without any modifiers that would show the meaning to be not the whole people but the determined enemies of Jesus. To the listener, it appears that the whole Jewish people stands against Jesus—and Jesus against the people. Pilate, on the other hand, is presented as the good Roman who would willingly have saved Jesus but was forced to give in to the threats of the mob. All of this has occasioned great folly and evil on the part of many—including preachers—not acquainted with the kind of writing this is and the circumstances that gave it birth. We now have directives from various Roman congregations that encourage homilists to be certain that the meaning behind the words is clear. Obviously, that approach is limited if the homily is to be more than a lesson about John's time and theology. The scripture scholar Raymond Brown (*Worship*, March 1975) argues that we should continue to read this narrative as it is written, but "once having read it, then to preach forcefully that such hostility between Christian and Jew cannot be continued today and is against our fundamental understanding of Christianity." He contends that it is time "to see that some attitudes found in the scriptures, however explicable in the times in which they originated, may be wrong attitudes if repeated today."

Another scholar, Gerard Sloyan, offers a different, somewhat more urgent, approach:

> The Passion according to John needs explanation before it is read or sung. It is a powerful piece, but if it is heard with the ears of modern history, its effect will be quite the opposite of that intended. Careful homiletic treatment should then *precede* it, even if none follows it. The homilist needs to have done hard study of the major themes of this gospel, which peak in chapters 18 and 19. The Johannine irony intended by Caiaphas's proposal that one man die for the people (18:14), the suggestion that ritual purity be avoided while this monstrous injustice is being carried out (18:28) and the meaning of "truth" and the double meaning of "king of Judea/the Jews"—all must be explored to help people know what to listen for, lest they think they are hearing mere history. (*Pastoral Music*, August/September 1989, page 18)

This problem will be altered somewhat with the introduction (probably in late 1993) of a revised lectionary. In the United States, this will introduce also a revised translation for lectionary use. One of the principles to be followed in this translation for the lectionary states:

> The expression "the Jews" in the Fourth Gospel is translated as "the Jewish authorities" or "the Jewish religious leaders" or "the Jewish

leaders" or the "Jewish people," etc., in accord with the *Guidelines on Religious Relations with the Jews* (December 1, 1974), of the Apostolic See's Council on Religious Relations with the Jews.

Is it worth this? It is. In our country, it is true that the reading of John's passion narrative is no longer the occasion for the Good Friday liturgy to be followed by bitter verbal and physical attacks against Jews, but such reading and the thoughtless preaching that occasionally follows it continue to create images in the minds of listeners. Such images are the stuff of today's anti-Semitism. The words and notions of John, so much at the heart of things for us at their best and so damaging at their worst, must be faced. Homilists will find guidance in *When Catholics Speak about Jews* by John T. Pawlikowski and James A. Wilde (LTP) and in the important work of the United States bishops' conference: *God's Mercy Endures Forever: Guidelines on the Presentation of Jews and Judaism in Catholic Preaching* (USCC Publications).

A homily and a time of silence follow the reading of the passion. The homilist should prepare by engaging all the scriptures of this day, the other important deeds of the ritual (interceding, venerating the cross) and the place of this moment in the observance of the whole Triduum. The homily is not a throw-away moment in the day's liturgy.

After the homily, the elect (and catechumens) are dismissed from the assembly. Although the eucharist is not celebrated, catechumens traditionally are dismissed before the intercessions (only after baptism does intercession become one's privilege and duty); nor do they have any role in the quiet communion rite of this liturgy. The words of dismissal should speak of our eagerness to be with the elect at the Easter Vigil and should exhort them to persevere in fasting and prayer, as will the faithful, and to return tomorrow (if this is part of the parish's Holy Saturday) to profess their faith through the recitation of the creed. On this day, no catechist would accompany the elect and the candidates as all the faithful would take part in the intercessions and the veneration of the cross. Later in the day, sponsors or catechists might come with individuals to venerate the cross.

The General Intercessions

The liturgy of the word concludes today as it does on Sunday with the prayers of intercession.

The prayers in the sacramentary follow the general order given in the *General Instruction of the Roman Missal* (#46) for these prayers: the church, public authorities and the salvation of the world, those oppressed by any need, the local community. Thus we have prayers for the church, for the pope, for the clergy and laity of the church, for those preparing for baptism, for the unity of Christians, for the Jewish people, for those who do not believe in Christ, for those who do not believe in God, for all in public office, for those in special need.

The ritual can become boring here if the passion was poorly proclaimed, the homily long and careless. Now come these prayers. It is hard work to establish a parish habit for this part of the liturgy, and more work each year for all the ministers involved, but that is what must happen. The dynamic presumed, of course, is of the passion so proclaimed (and perhaps, through song, participated in) and a homily so engaging that the assembly now stands eager to do this task of interceding. At this assembly in the midst of Triduum, there seems no task more worthy of our time than this.

If Sunday by Sunday the parish knows about this work of interceding, then that is possible. The restoration of the general intercessions in the Sunday eucharist has not gone all that well. An assembly still may not have a sense that we are baptized to do this work, this reminding God of the troubles in this world. The intercessions at each Sunday's liturgy are rehearsal for all the baptized: We are charged to keep these things—church, leaders, the poor, the oppressed, the local community—constantly in mind and to make as certain as we can that God also keeps them in mind. Such work requires a strong ritual form, a powerful litany in many cases, that will catch us up in intercession.

Today, though, we do our intercessions in another ancient form: the call to remember and pray for someone, then silence for reflection so that each call may take shape in our hearts, then the voicing of our prayer by the presider and the assembly's "Amen" to what has been said. And, like a litany, the pattern repeats.

What goes wrong with this pattern most often is simply haste. The leaders are in a hurry to get through this because they believe the assembly won't stand still too long. And the sense of hurry is counterproductive: It makes the prayers seem very long to the assembly—because they catch no sense of why we are doing this, of the urgency or sweep of the prayer. Pace—not slowness—is crucial.

Equally important is a good pattern to be used for each intercession. One voice calls to prayer ("Let us pray . . ."). This is the role of the deacon, if there is one today; otherwise, it should be a woman's voice when the presider, who will chant or read the prayer that concludes each intercession, is a man. These two leaders must rehearse each prayer, working on tone of voice, speed, expression and especially pacing. Before this, those preparing the liturgies must examine the pattern the parish uses to be sure it works. Where do the leaders stand? How does the one who announces the intercession direct these words (remember that they are not prayers, they are more like a summons) to the assembly? Are these announcements of the intentions sung or spoken? How is the silent time handled? If there is kneeling (with or without the spoken invitation), is it long enough for quiet to settle in, or are we just jumping down and up? If there is no kneeling (and that is better than a rushed genuflection), then what is there to give a flow and rhythm to the assembly's participation in these prayers?

Is there, as the sacramentary suggests, an acclamation that the assembly sings before or after the silence that follows the announcement of each intercession? What is the cue for this acclamation? How is the prayer itself to be sung or spoken? Will the "Amen" be sung well if the prayer is sung?

What of the prayers themselves? Those in the sacramentary are very heavy on praying for the church, very light on the world. One rubric in the sacramentary seems to allow for some rearrangement: "The priest may choose from the prayers in the missal those which are more appropriate to local circumstances, provided the series follows the rule for the general intercessions." That rule is simply the one of order: church, leaders, the poor, the local community. Those wishing to pursue this option then would study the various prayers found in the sacramentary under "Masses and Prayers for Various Needs and Occasions." These include prayers, for example, for peace and justice, in time of war, for productive land, for those who suffer from famine, for refugees and exiles, for prisoners, for the sick, for the family and for many more. Some are excellent texts, some weak. In any case, if a few of these were chosen for use (and some of those given in the sacramentary were omitted), the new prayers would need appropriate announcements ("Let us pray for . . ."). These should be of the same tone and quality as those in the sacramentary. Which sacramentary prayers could be omitted? Certainly not the prayer for the church or for those preparing for baptism; and we seldom pray for Christian unity and almost never pray for the Jewish people, so those should remain. We have a strong tradition, even an obligation, to pray for those in public office and for those with great needs, though these might take various forms today.

Surely, the rule here is not to replace a good text with a poor one, not to replace a universal prayer with one that is too particular, not to lose the breadth these prayers seek. Not all new texts are better than the ones offered in the sacramentary, but by the same standard, several of those in the sacramentary are hardly up to the burden of these prayers.

The preparation of this rite should attend first to a good order and pace and to participation through listening, acclaiming and posture. After that, attention can be paid to the texts with a strong prejudice for the offerings in the sacramentary. (Note that the 1988 *Circular Letter* seems to suggest that the substitution of other prayers from the sacramentary is to be done only when the bishop has permitted or prescribed the adding of special intentions [#67].) The revised sacramentary, expected in the mid-1990s, should provide a better selection of texts for these prayers.

This is the climax of the liturgy today, yet like the mandatum yesterday, it is (almost entirely) without words. All the words belong to the assembly, as does the movement of the procession.

The origins of this ritual probably are in fourth-century Jerusalem. The relic of the cross would be held by the bishop and the faithful would come forward to bow and touch the cross with their foreheads, then their eyes, then their lips. This ritual slowly spread. At first, the veneration was directed toward a relic of the true cross; only much later was this replaced by an image of the cross and later yet, in some places, by the crucifix. (See articles by Patrick Regan in *Worship* [January 1978] and in *Liturgy: The Holy Cross* [The Liturgical Conference, 1980].)

The question of what cross or crucifix to use should be brought up only if the parish never has established a single good practice. If the practice has been to pull out a convenient crucifix, something hardly seen the rest of the year and of no particular beauty, then it is well to consider some change. But if the practice has been to venerate the parish's principal image of the cross (even if this is a crucifix), the image that is present year-round in the assembly or the image that is carried into the assembly in procession each Sunday, then there is no call to change.

Speaking in the abstract, a wooden cross (without corpus) seems the best choice. Cross is suggested rather than crucifix because the church is not looking here at a picture. The church holds up and gazes at the cross. The crucifix would narrow on a moment in history; that is important but is not the need here. Even a crucifix with the image of the victorious Christ is not what we seek. The simple cross embraces the whole of the paschal mystery: Christ has died; Christ is risen; Christ will come again.

Also, the preference—again speaking in the abstract—must be for wood. The poetry of liturgy and tradition are filled with this and there seems no good reason not to honor it. The acclamation is: Behold the *wood* of the cross. That in itself might not be so

The Veneration of the Cross

important were it not for the way the church has spoken in songs and antiphons of the cross as a tree, of the wood of the cross as the tree of life and the ark where life was saved in the flood and the firewood prepared for Abraham's sacrifice and the wood of Moses' staff—and on and on.

There is here, in this preference for a cross made of wood, nothing about Good Friday and the veneration that could not be said of the processional cross, that standard that leads the assembly into its rituals and that stands in the midst of the community throughout those rites. But to repeat: If the parish has established a tradition, especially one using its own main image of the cross, the presumption would be in favor of maintaining the local custom.

Showing the Cross

The assembly remains standing after the intercessions. The sacramentary offers two forms for the first moments of the veneration. In the first form, the veiled cross is carried from its place directly to the area near the altar. There the presider receives the cross and lifts it up. In three stages, the veil is removed. After each stage, the acclamation is sung by presider (or cantor) and assembly, after each of which the assembly kneels for a brief time.

In the second form, the presider and acolytes go to the church door and take the cross (which has not been veiled). They enter the assembly with the cross held high; candles (and incense) can precede the cross. The cross is lifted up from first one and then another place within the assembly, and finally a third time near the altar. Each time the acclamation is sung by presider (or cantor) and assembly, after which the assembly kneels for a brief time.

If the cross has in fact been present in the area since the Triduum began (as was suggested previously in the notes on Holy Thursday as appropriate in some circumstances), either of these forms of veneration can still be used. Carrying the cross into the midst of the assembly is not an essential part of the ritual. Acclaiming the cross is what matters, then venerating it.

As to which form is to be chosen, if the unveiling has been traditional, many people will associate it with Good Friday and it should be maintained. If there is not that sense, then the second form probably is better for it will be echoed in the entrance of the paschal candle; also, with the unveiled cross, full attention can be given to the cross itself, not to the process of unveiling it. There is one practical problem, though, with the second form. In churches with pews and kneelers, people may be able to turn and look at the cross (as they are summoned to do: "Behold the wood of the cross . . ."), but they cannot kneel down facing the cross. It can be awkward and distracting. There are two possible solutions. First, the kneeling can be omitted after the first two acclamations when the station is somewhere in the main aisle of the church. Then a longer time of kneeling can take place after the third acclamation (from the area near the altar, when the assembly is facing forward). Or second, the procession can so use the space that each of the three positions is somewhere in front of the whole assembly, thus allowing all to kneel each time without turning around.

Whichever form is used, note that the 1988 *Circular Letter* speaks in strong terms of this rite:

> The cross for the showing should be large and beautiful and one of the two formularies provided in the Missal is to be used. The rite should be carried out with a splendor in keeping with this great mystery of our salvation: both the invitation made in showing the cross and the response of the people are to be sung and as the priest stands holding the elevated cross the reverential silence after each prostration is not to be omitted. (#68)

The words "carried out with the splendor" do not indicate grandeur but rather dignity and enthusiastic participation.

Incense as well as candles can be carried by acolytes in the procession and held beside the cross during the acclamation and kneeling, then placed near the cross during the time of the procession. The incense can be in thuribles or in bowls; it should be chosen especially for this day. Its sweetness or bittersweetness becomes part of the ritual experience of the Triduum. Note how the poetry of the church uses *dulcis,* sweet, so often to describe this cross, this wood. The incense is placed on the coals only when the procession with the cross takes shape; the bowls might remain by the cross as the liturgy concludes, and more incense could be added periodically until the coals have burned out.

If, as discussed earlier, the young children were sent to another place for their liturgy of the word, they should return in this procession; after the third acclamation of the cross, they go to join their families.

Coming Forward to the Cross

After the third acclamation, the assembly remains kneeling. The ministers hold the cross in such a way that it may be venerated by all, one at a time, and the procession begins. Usually, the ministers come first, but this is not necessary. In some places, the cross is laid on the floor (on a carpet or on flowers put down for this purpose) rather than held by ministers. The cross should never be positioned leaning against some furniture or the altar or propped up in any way that distracts from its beauty.

Local practices for the individual veneration of the cross vary greatly and most of them should be respected. One that is not to be respected is the multiplication of crosses. The sacramentary itself is clear: only one cross. But the addenda for the United States do allow a second or third cross. This never should be the choice. The *Circular Letter* affirms the sacramentary's preference:

> Only one cross should be used for the veneration, as is required for the authenticity of this sign. (#69)

The sacramentary suggests that if the size of the assembly would mean a long, long time in individual veneration of the cross, then after a number of people (representing all the parish) have come forward, the cross again can be lifted up for all to see; the assembly kneels for some moments. After the liturgy, the cross may be venerated throughout the evening and on Saturday. (What the sacramentary actually says is: "If the number of people makes it impossible for everyone to venerate the cross individually . . ." "Impossible" is a strong word.)

At any rate, such efficiency should be avoided. Experience has shown that people are not in a hurry today. We have nothing else to do but this. And it is a sung ritual, which can make a great difference to the perception of time and to the way the time enriches us. The number of appropriate antiphons, hymns and other pieces—from long tradition or more recently composed—provide for participation of all in some singing and in some listening to choir and cantor. All of the words sung should be drawn from the spirit of this day's liturgy and, in turn, should build that spirit. At the same time, there should be a sense of freedom so that individuals who wish to leave after venerating the cross may do so. Nothing needs to be said; people know this. Rarely then would it be necessary to shorten the time of veneration; all present should be able to come forward to the one cross.

Because there is only one cross, the manner of coming forward will be different than that of communion on Sunday when there are several communion stations. Ushers should be included in the rehearsal so that this can take place without confusion. Some would argue that the spirit of these moments would suggest letting people move forward on their own, not as part of a row-by-row procession. That may work where there is more spacious seating, but not where people sit in pews or tight rows of chairs. Besides, a procession and not simply a queue is exactly the image that is needed here.

Some parishes with large numbers in attendance have worked hard at the choreography of this procession. They have used a very large wooden cross. People stream to it (again, another good image for the action here) from several directions, and three or four people may venerate the cross at once because of its size.

Individuals do not have to conform to any one way of venerating the cross. Some may genuflect, some bow, some touch the wood, some kiss it, some simply pause before it. There should be a sense of freedom and no rushing. Those who come forward first might be asked by the ushers before the liturgy begins to give good examples of the several ways that individuals might choose to venerate the cross. Or the ushers themselves might venerate the cross at the same time as the other ministers, themselves giving this example, then tending to the procession. In this way, there is a freedom for everyone that follows and, for those that need it, a "vocabulary" of gestures. Like so much that we do in the Triduum, this gesture of veneration could appropriately be reflected on in a homily during

Eastertime. That is what mystagogia means: to unfold the depth and strength of these rites.

In 1989, the *Sourcebook for Sundays and Seasons* (LTP) contained some suggestions concerning the former rubric that called for the ministers to remove their shoes before venerating the cross:

> A beautiful, powerful gesture on this day is for all ministers—indeed, all the people—to come to the cross barefoot or in stocking feet. This type of tradition happens over years, but begins with preparation during Lent. It calls to mind several images: Isn't the holy cross like the burning bush? Isn't this place holy ground? Read the powerful words of Song of Songs 5:2–8. We have removed our shoes and washed our feet, a preparation for entering the bath of baptism!

This direction about removing one's shoes remains a part of the *Ceremonial of Bishops*. The 1992 *Sourcebook* suggests:

> That rubrical book calls for the presider to leave chasuble and shoes at the chair. They should be taken off before the entrance of the cross, so that the procession flows into the veneration. This tradition, observed by many monastic orders and mentioned by ancient writers, catches on quickly—if the presider and other assisting ministers handle it with grace. Announce it in the participation booklet or in a brief verbal invitation. If the presider is seen taking shoes off while others in the sanctuary do the same, the assembly will feel comfortable removing their shoes.

There is an extravagance here, an attention, a shared gesture that goes beyond what we usually expect. It may be what we need.

Music for the Veneration

The strongest possible music should be chosen for the initial acclamation of the cross. Some have used settings of the "Holy is God, holy and strong, holy immortal one, have mercy on us." This is the key text of the veneration (especially with the Greek and Latin acclamations). It unites the church over centuries and across East and West. There are several musical settings. It could be repeated between other hymns and antiphons during the time of the veneration. In this way, even if the length of the veneration seems to demand a number of texts rather than the ideal single composition, the recurrence of some one key melody and text will give the rite unity.

The music that fills the time of the veneration then would be drawn from the many texts and melodies that proclaim the mystery of the cross. Instruments should be used, if at all, only to support the singing. Some pieces might be for choir alone, but the assembly never should be silent for too long. Styles can vary from the reflective ostinato music of Taizé (if "Jesus, remember me" or "Adoramus te, Christe" or "Crucem tuam" was used at the end of the Thursday liturgy, it can be repeated now and perhaps again with the Vigil, binding together the days) to traditional hymns with chant or other tunes (again, the "Vexilla Regis" would be almost necessary).

The argument about the use of Reproaches continues as to whether their history and their use are anti-Semitic. They have been eliminated by some churches and discouraged by others. Even apart from the distasteful way they seem to play Jesus against the Jewish people, it is difficult to understand how these texts would be desirable in the liturgy of Good Friday. Many better choices are available to us. The annual *Sourcebook for Sundays and Seasons* (LTP) presents a brief listing of some of these. The first texts given in the sacramentary for the veneration of the cross might well be a measure for others to be chosen for singing today:

> We worship you, Lord.
> We venerate your cross.
> We praise your resurrection.
> Through the cross you brought joy to the world.

Those who prepare this rite, and especially those who search for its music, might begin by reflecting on the words to some of the hymns about the cross mentioned previously and on other texts from our tradition. Some of the latter are found in *A Triduum Sourcebook* (LTP), pages 17, 31 and 51–54.

The Communion Rite

Until the reforms of the 1950s, communion was received only by the presider at this liturgy. In the more ancient observances of the days leading to the Vigil, no one received communion on this day, but from the seventh to the thirteenth centuries, some churches used bread consecrated on the previous day for the communion of the faithful. At present, Good Friday rightly has no eucharist, but it has this holy communion at the conclusion of this liturgy. Perhaps the future will see a return to the earliest practice, where we fast altogether from the sacraments from the time we enter the Triduum until the Vigil. For now, the nature of the Good Friday liturgy suggests that the communion rite be very simple. Without any ceremony or procession, the bread consecrated Thursday evening is brought into the assembly. Two acolytes with lighted candles accompany the deacon or presider; the candles are placed on or near the altar, on which a cloth now has been placed.

If additional ministers of communion are needed, it would seem best that they go with the deacon or presider to bring in the bread, and that each carry a vessel into the assembly; there is no provision in the rite for a time to place bread from the one vessel into many; it should be done beforehand.

In the usual way, the presider invites all to pray the Our Father. The *Circular Letter* presumes that this will be sung, but there should be some question about this. If it is not customary to sing the Our Father on Sunday, then singing it today would be the wrong message entirely, as if this communion rite had more solemnity here than at the Sunday celebration.

The presider continues, "Deliver us . . ." and the assembly concludes with the usual acclamation. The presider then speaks the invitation to communion (only the presider, not other communion ministers, should hold a piece of the bread), "This is the Lamb of God . . ." and all respond. The presider takes communion and immediately the ministers begin the communion of the assembly.

Many would suggest rather quiet singing during communion, perhaps repeating the music used on Thursday. Certainly, the communion song should not be one that focuses on the meal itself, the banquet, the bread and wine. This communion service is detached from the eucharist. The singing could have the same content and tone as the singing during the procession to the cross.

After communion, one of the ministers takes the remaining bread from the church to a suitable place. If the church has a tabernacle in it, this is not used; it remains empty. Almost all the bread should be consumed here by the ministers; only what is needed for viaticum is to remain. Communion to the sick is not permitted on Holy Saturday.

After a silent time, all stand and the presider speaks or chants the prayer that begins "Almighty and eternal God." Note that this is not, in the usual sense, a prayer after communion. This is followed by the prayer over the people ("Lord, send down your abundant blessing").

There is nothing after the "Amen" to this prayer. Silence should be observed by ministers and by all as they depart. The best practice is for the ministers not to leave in procession. They may approach and bow to the cross, then some take a place in the assembly to continue in prayer. Some leave. Some may kneel for a while near the cross. One may move the communion candles nearer to the cross. The lights are dimmed. The whole sense is that the church continues in vigiling and prayer.

The cross should remain completely approachable from now on. Candles and incense can be burning there. Texts from scripture along with prayers and hymns can be made available near the cross. When possible, the vigiling continues throughout the night. The liturgy of the hours can be prayed at appropriate times.

Other Rites of Thursday Night, Friday and Saturday

A parish's life in the Triduum has many sides: the all-embracing ways that these days are known and kept by parishioners; the worthy celebration of the Vigil and the principal rites of Thursday night and Friday; the development or the beginning of a tradition for smaller gatherings for various rites that are possible during these days. Here we will discuss some of these.

The first rubric of the sacramentary for Good Friday is clear and strong: "According to the church's ancient tradition, the sacraments are not celebrated today or tomorrow." Those who have some responsibility from year to year for the integrity of these days need a practical sense for what this means:

- The funeral Mass is not celebrated (this includes Holy Thursday also and, of course, Easter Sunday); see #178 and #179 of the *Order of Christian Funerals*.

- Communion may be taken to the sick on Holy Thursday and on Good Friday, but on Holy Saturday communion may be given before the Vigil only as viaticum. A parish should consider the ways in which those who are sick or in hospitals or in prison or homebound can be joined to the keeping of the Triduum. Certainly, this would be in holy communion brought from the Mass of Easter Sunday. Communion on Holy Thursday was discussed earlier: The suggestion is that the sick and others be visited on Good Friday and Holy Saturday and that the visitors, if appropriate, bring some reading of scripture and some part of the church's prayer during the Triduum to all those unable to be present.

- Communal penance services are part of our lenten practice and do not belong anywhere in the Triduum; many would argue that all individual confessions also should be completed before the Triduum begins.

- Weddings are not celebrated from Holy Thursday to Easter Sunday.

- The anointing of a sick person normally would be scheduled, except for emergencies, for a time before or after the Triduum.

Many dioceses have their own pastoral directives for the celebration of the sacraments during the whole paschal season. In particular, some dioceses emphasize that the initiation sacraments of baptism (including infant baptism), confirmation and first eucharist are not appropriate during Lent. The celebration of marriage also is not encouraged during this penitential season.

It will be a familiar but frustrating path if Catholic parishes choose to dwell on the regulations and their exceptions. These regulations are a way to embody that which is central: From Thursday night until after the Vigil, the church fasts from the sacraments. Such a practice makes sense only when our understanding of weddings, burials, anointings, penance and all the rest is thoroughly ecclesial. They are deeds done by this church. And during Lent, with a building intensity, and completely during the Triduum, the church is bound up in the hard work of repentance and initiation. That intense and recurring focus is not unrelated to letting Eastertime be the great time of abundance when marriages are celebrated, the sick are anointed (often in the midst of the church), children complete their initiation in confirmation and first communion. These first 48 hours of the Triduum with their various forms of fasting, including this fast from the sacraments, never will make sense apart from the Vigil and the sacramental life that overflows into all of Eastertime.

In planning its various times of prayer, a parish will be guided by its overall sense for the Triduum as well as by the character of the days and hours that lead up to the Vigil. We have seen that Thursday night, after the liturgy of entrance into the Triduum, invites a continued vigiling that is centered briefly at the chapel with the

Character of These Days

reserved sacrament, but continues in the church. And Friday morning is filled with an awareness of the solemn liturgy of the passion; the very hours of the morning and early afternoon mark times familiar from the passion narrative. The afternoon liturgy itself, with the veneration of the cross, leaves the cross in the midst of the church as the tree of life; this mingles with the image of the Lord's burial as we observe Friday evening.

Holy Saturday

That evening blends into Saturday as the second full day of the Triduum. This day, which logically would be the strongest hours of anticipation, often seems without character. This will come as the Vigil takes a stronger hold in parish life, but even as that is happening, those involved as parish staff, liturgical ministers, sponsors and catechists with the catechumenate should be invited to ponder the beauty of this Holy Saturday and so share it with the larger parish.

What is this beauty? Saturday, the seventh day of creation, is the day of rest, and that has been the image that centers the church's prayer this day. It is the day of the burial and rest of the Lord. The church often has dwelt with a verse of Psalm 4: "In peace, I will lie down and sleep." The sacramentary says, "On Holy Saturday, the church waits at the Lord's tomb, meditating on his suffering and death."

At Saturday's Office of Readings, the church reads chapter 4 of the Letter to the Hebrews:

> A sabbath rest still remains for the people of God; for those who enter God's rest also cease from their labors as God did. Let us therefore make every effort to enter that rest.

To enter God's rest—that is something of what this day is to be about. That is why all preparations and rehearsals for the Vigil were concluded before the Triduum began. That is why also by encouragement and especially by example all parishioners are urged to make this a quiet and peaceful day. The scheduling of various times of prayer can contribute to this, but we need more than this if we are to evolve a tradition in which families with young children, singles, the elderly, the workaholics and the unemployed can find themselves at peace and at rest this day. Half hours and hours of vigiling in the church can continue until the Vigil itself begins after dark.

In some traditions, especially in the Eastern churches, the few scripture verses that speak of the burial of Christ and of the descent into hell (1 Peter 4:6, "the gospel proclaimed even to the dead," and 3:19, "he went and made a proclamation to the spirits in prison," and Ephesians 4:9, "he first descended into the lower parts of the earth") have been the source of much preaching and song about Holy Saturday. Most of us know little of this and probably tend to take it too literally, missing the very core of this tradition. That core becomes the great Easter song of the Orthodox church: Christ has by death trampled down death. That song is what is welling up in the church through Holy Saturday.

When we profess in the Apostles' Creed, "He descended to the dead," we have the words for this tradition. What matters is not the physics but the faith: In death and burial, Christ has defeated all that we mean by "death." When the church has attempted to make this more vivid, it only wants to get at something without which we will not understand what happens tonight beside and within the font. Some of the Orthodox texts may help to convey this understanding of Holy Saturday:

> O Christ, you slept a life-giving sleep in the grave,
> and you awakened humankind from the heavy sleep of sin.

> O Lord, my God, I sing unto you a burial song and a funeral chant, who by your burial have opened for me a door to life, and by your death have brought an end to death and hell.

> Today Hades tearfully sighs: "Would that I had not received him who was born of Mary, for he came to me and destroyed my power; he broke my bronze gates, and being God, delivered the souls I had been holding captive." O Lord, glory to your cross and to your holy resurrection!

All of this elaborates on the scripture verse we hear in the Roman liturgy of the hours today: "O Death, I will be your death. O Grave,

I will be your destruction." But all of this is also a spelling out of the spirit of this day that most of us know only slightly, as we meet it, for example, in the Easter sequence, "Mors et vita duello . . .":

> Death and life have contended in that combat stupendous:
> The prince of life, who died, reigns immortal.

There is perhaps a storybook quality to such language that may distance it from our lives. Removing that distance is a task of ritual and reflection and preaching, on Holy Saturday and during the Easter-time also. What is at stake here is this: Even as we regain the presence of adult initiation in our parishes, we are in danger of losing how baptism is death, for each of us, day after day after day. It is a struggle, but our victory is sealed in Christ's victory. That is the "spirituality" that the church's liturgy would hand on to us to work out in these times. This spirit, so much the essence of Holy Saturday, is obviously not in harmony with the times. These seemingly contradictory things are somehow to fill our Holy Saturday observance—a burial and a Sabbath rest that are at the very same time seizing life from death and hell itself.

Times of Gathering

If the parish's schedule these days looks something like a monastic routine or a retreat, that is not far from what is needed. The constant prayer of the church, including the presence of some persons at all hours in the church, rises up at various times as small or large numbers gather to pray. The tradition of the church, as well as various rubrics and directives, would tell us that in planning this, certain priorities should be followed. In most parishes, some elements already are in place. More might be desirable. Those things that are in place should be evaluated in light of the demands made by the Triduum and different hours within it. One other criterion is important: Nothing should be scheduled to detract from the importance of the principal liturgies of these days. In every presentation—even the simple matter of how the parish schedule appears on a page—these liturgies should be seen as the primary gatherings of the parish.

When those liturgies have been given their place and attention, certain priorities may be used in deciding what else is possible. (We

are speaking here of the time from Thursday night to the Vigil. If the whole of the Triduum were under consideration, first priority would go to the celebration of Vespers on Easter Sunday evening. See the notes in the chapter "Easter Sunday.")

First, the Preparation Rites on Holy Saturday. These final rites before baptism include the "return" or recitation of the creed, the ephphetha rite and perhaps the choosing of a baptismal name. (If the presentation of the Lord's Prayer was not done earlier, it also can be done on Holy Saturday.) The RCIA, #185, notes that these take place during a time when the elect have gathered for reflection and prayer.

Second, the liturgy of the hours. Given the times of the principal liturgies, Morning Prayer on Friday and Saturday are most needed, but there also is Night Prayer on Thursday and Friday, Midday Prayer on Friday and Saturday and Evening Prayer on Saturday. The Office of Readings also is part of the liturgy of the hours; its texts, and others that might be added, are a resource for giving greater length and substance to any of these times, but particularly to Morning Prayer.

Third, other devotions. Some of these already may be part of the parish's keeping of the Triduum: for example, devotions before the Blessed Sacrament on Thursday night, stations of the cross, traditional devotions associated with the burial and tomb of Christ, the blessing of Easter foods.

These priorities, rather than the chronology of the days themselves, will govern the brief descriptions that follow.

First Priority: Preparation Rites on Holy Saturday

The RCIA notes in #185 that this is a day of prayer, fasting and reflection for the elect. If possible, they are to spend some of this time together. Their sponsors and other members of the parish should be invited to be present also, but this is not a "social" time in any way. The atmosphere should be one of silence or perhaps of some shared reflection on the psalms and scriptures of the day's prayer.

Those who prepare the liturgy can find much help in #186 through #205 of the RCIA. In most parishes in this country, the suggestion in #186 will form the order of the service: "When both the recitation of the creed and the ephphetha rite are celebrated, the ephphetha rite immediately precedes the 'Prayer before the Recitation.'" A model for the celebration of the Preparation Rites then is given in #187 through #192. The sense here is that this rite is to take some time; Holy Saturday is a day without hurry.

In the 1992 *Sourcebook for Sundays and Seasons* (LTP), Thomas Ryan suggests that there is another area of concern when preparing this rite. If infants are to be baptized at the Vigil, it almost certainly will be desirable to gather the infants, parents and godparents on Holy Saturday and celebrate the preparatory elements from the rite of infant baptism. Ryan proposes the following structure for a rite that includes both infants and the elect. This is included for those parishes that have decided to baptize infants at the Vigil. Many would argue that only infant children of adults who are being baptized should be included, and that Easter Sunday or a following Sunday is best for all other infant baptisms.

- Gathering hymn with the entire assembly at the entranceway.

- Rite of receiving the infants (with texts and action of signing from the *Rite of Baptism for Children* [RBC], #35–41).

- Procession of all, with an appropriate refrain or a well-known hymn sung by all, to the place where they will be seated.

- Psalms and scripture of the appropriate hour of the day or the proclamation of one or two of the scriptures listed in the Preparation of the Elect (RCIA, #179–80, #194, #198).

- Homily.

- Preparation rites for the infants: prayer of exorcism (RBC, #49) and, possibly, the anointing with the oil of catechumens (RBC, #50).

- Preparation rites for the elect (adults and also children of catechetical age): one or more of the rites listed in RCIA, #185.2.

- Singing of a hymn or of a gospel canticle (if this rite is part of Morning Prayer or Evening Prayer).

- Prayer of Blessing (RCIA, #204).

- Dismissal (RCIA, #205).

Some attention might be given to the suggestion made in RCIA, #200, that there should be a focus on the names of the elect (and of the infants also). In most cases, this will not be a new name, but the given name in which the person will be baptized. The suggestion in the rite is that there should be an explanation of the given name of each of the elect. Perhaps this could be built into the homily along with some reference to the great litany of the saints that will be heard at the Vigil. Year after year, such attention would give the sense for the Christian importance of a name: That by our names we are known and loved and inscribed by God for life.

The RCIA further suggests in #185.2 that when the presentation of the Lord's Prayer has not occurred, it be done on this day. Where the elect have been dismissed regularly at Sunday eucharist, the Lord's Prayer would be given to them today as immediate preparation for their first participation in the eucharist and holy communion of the church. This is an entire rite (RCIA, #178–83), but if done today, combined with the return of the creed, it would be but one simple element within the larger ritual. The rite, of course, gathers up what has happened: the way that sponsor, godparent, catechist and the whole community have been teaching Catholic prayer to the elect.

In the rites of giving the church's creed and the church's prayer to the elect, we are presenting the spoken words of the faithful to those soon to be baptized. This is not a matter of handing over a scroll of written words, but words on the lips of believers. Any giving of the Lord's Prayer or the creed in written form should be done apart from the rite.

Should such a gathering with the elect be the occasion for any rehearsal of the baptism rite of the Vigil? First of all, no rehearsals should take place today, for anyone. But second, the ancient practice of the church was that the elect know almost nothing about what would take place at the Vigil. They are told what garments they need to bring and little more (see Don Neumann's suggestions in *Holy Week in the Parish*, Liturgical Press, page 37). Godparents and others should attend a rehearsal prior to the Triduum so that they can be of real assistance to the elect at the liturgy. During Eastertime, the newly baptized will be led to explore all the richness of the Vigil.

What will motivate parishioners to be part of these Holy Saturday rites? This is a matter of the growing effect of a good practice of initiation, in all its phases, in the parish. As parishioners see the catechumens dismissed, as they witness the election and the scrutiny rites, as many parishioners occasionally have direct contact with the catechumens and elect, the motives for attendance are created. The parish schedule for the Triduum can try to add some urgency to this, explaining that on Saturday those we have accompanied this close to baptism will make their final preparation. Attendance is also a matter of the catechesis about and example of the keeping of these days. Special efforts might be made to invite those who were baptized in previous years to be present.

Parishes with some experience of the liturgy of the hours, especially of Evening Prayer (perhaps on the Sundays of Advent and Lent), already will know something of the content and order of the church's prayer. They also know that even small numbers of parishioners can celebrate these rites with great power, provided adequate preparation of the space, music, ministries and participation aids has been done. Note that the 1988 *Circular Letter* says in #40 that the bishop "should, if possible, take part with the people and clergy in the cathedral church." (This reinforces recommendations in the *Ceremonial of Bishops*.)

The basic resource is the *Liturgy of the Hours* with the orders of service presented there for the following times of prayer:

- Night Prayer on Thursday
- Morning Prayer on Friday
- Daytime Prayer on Friday (with some texts designated for Midmorning, Midday or Midafternoon)
- Night Prayer on Friday
- Morning Prayer on Saturday
- Daytime Prayer on Saturday (with some texts designated for Midmorning, Midday or Midafternoon)
- Evening Prayer on Saturday

Second Priority: The Liturgy of the Hours

If there is a core of people, presumably the parish staff, commit-ted to keeping the Triduum, and if the busyness of preparing the main liturgies has been handled before Thursday evening, then several or even all of these times of prayer can become part of the parish schedule. It is not at all a matter of numbers, then, but a matter of knowing that this core group will be present and that the rites will be well carried out.

The place of these rites is the church. Before the main liturgy of Good Friday, those praying the liturgy of the hours can assemble in the empty space near the altar or in another appropriate place. Only a few lighted candles are present; nothing else is needed. Between the Good Friday afternoon liturgy and the Easter Vigil, the place for the assembly can be around the cross. Again, there are only the lighted candles (and perhaps new coals can be lighted beforehand and some incense added).

Sitting audience-fashion in pews, even if people will come together in one section, does not work well. Two rows of chairs, facing each other, or a circle of chairs is much more effective.

The *Circular Letter* makes one recommendation concerning the environment of the church on Holy Saturday that might be considered:

> An image of Christ hanging on the cross or resting in the tomb or descending into hell, which expresses the mystery of Holy Saturday, as well as an image of his sorrowing Mother may be set out in the church for veneration by the faithful.

The suggestion is not to multiply images. In most places, the cross would best remain the single image throughout this day. But there may be churches where an icon of great beauty, a candle burning beside it, could focus both the individual prayers and these times of gathering for the liturgy of the hours. Icons that bear great weight in the Eastern churches, however, will not automatically bring that with them. If the parish possesses a worthy icon of the descent into hell, some effort should be made beforehand, or in a short homily at Morning Prayer, for example, to speak of the image (the Holy

Saturday reading on page 100, for example, would be a possible reflection on this image).

For each time the liturgy of the hours is celebrated, clear and attractive participation aids should be provided with the psalms and other texts needed by the participants. These are saved and used each year.

The order of prayer found in the *Liturgy of the Hours* can be followed; appropriate hymns can be chosen from the parish repertory. Psalms can be chanted or spoken. One of the basic elements of the liturgy in these days is the scriptural text that is recited from Holy Thursday until the Vigil. On Thursday it is simply:

> For our sake, Christ was obedient, accepting even death.

On Friday it becomes:

> For our sake, Christ was obedient, accepting even death, death on a cross.

And on Saturday it becomes:

> For our sake, Christ was obedient, accepting even death, death on a cross. Therefore God raised him on high and gave him the name above all other names.

Those preparing these rites certainly will need to make judgments about the length and complexity of the prayer. They decide what is to be recited and what is to be sung, how the psalms will be handled (alternating verses one side against another, or all together, or the cantor singing verses and the assembly singing the antiphon), which parts will be taken by the presider, at what times there is to be silence. In places where the liturgy of the hours is already done at other seasons, much of this will come easily. Once this is done, participation aids are prepared. Those who will lead (presider, cantor, lector) come together for a simple rehearsal. The ministry of presider should be shared among women and men in the parish who have shown readiness for this. In rehearsing, the ministers must determine a pace that is not rushed but allows for attention and reflection.

Some parishes will want to add to the previously mentioned list of times the Office of Readings. This has no assigned time of its own (it is an adaptation of the old Matins, or prayer during the night). One element of the Office of Readings should not be overlooked. On Good Friday and Holy Saturday, this Office contains readings that present the mysteries of these days in a way that still speaks to us. Both are from the preaching of the early centuries: Friday from John Chrysostom, Saturday from an unknown homilist. Chrysostom's homily is about the water and the blood from the side of Christ:

> There flowed from his side water and blood. Beloved, do not pass over this mystery without thought; it has yet another hidden meaning, which I will explain to you. I said that water and blood symbolized baptism and the holy eucharist. From these two sacraments the church is born: from baptism, the cleansing water that gives rebirth and renewal through the Holy Spirit, and from the holy eucharist. Since the symbols of baptism and the eucharist flowed from his side, it was from his side that Christ fashioned the church, as he had fashioned Eve from the side of Adam. Moses gives a hint of this when he tells the story of the first man and makes him exclaim: Bone from my bones and flesh from my flesh. . . . God took a rib when Adam was in a deep sleep, and in the same way Christ gave us the blood and the water after his own death. Do you understand, then, how Christ has united his bride to himself and what food he gives us all to eat? By one and the same food we are both brought into being and nourished. As a woman nourishes her child with her own blood and milk, so does Christ unceasingly nourish with his own blood those to whom he himself has given life.

The Saturday homily from the Office of Readings is a marvelous imagining of the victory that is ours over death:

> Something strange is happening—there is a great silence on earth today, a great silence and stillness. The whole earth keeps silence because the King is asleep. The earth trembled and is still because God has fallen asleep in the flesh and he has raised up all who have slept ever since the world began. . . . Greatly desiring to visit those who live in darkness and in the shadow of death, the Lord has gone to free from sorrow the captives Adam and Eve, he who is both God and son of Eve. The Lord

approached them bearing the cross, the weapon that had won him
the victory. At the sight of him, Adam struck his breast in terror and
cried out to everyone: "My Lord be with you all." Christ answered
him: "And with your spirit." He took him by the hand and raised
him up, saying, "Awake, O sleeper, and rise from the dead, and
Christ will give you light. . . . Rise, let us leave this place, for you
are in me and I am in you; together we form only one person and we
cannot be separated. . . . For the sake of you, who left a garden, I
was betrayed in a garden and crucified in a garden. See on my face
the spittle I received in order to restore to you the life I once breathed
into you. . . . See my hands, nailed firmly to a tree, for you who
once wickedly stretched out your hand to a tree. . . . The sword
that pierced me has sheathed the sword that was turned against you.
Rise, let us leave this place. . . . The bridal dwelling chamber is
adorned, the banquet is ready, the eternal dwelling places are
prepared, the treasure houses of all good things lie open."

It is not our style today, but there is something here so basic, so alive
in the images of scripture, so unafraid of those images and the reality
they convey! (Imagine this meeting: There is the shocked Adam
saying, "Dominus tecum," to Christ, and the latter responding like
an acolyte, "Et cum spiritu tuo." Playfulness is part of today's
deathly seriousness.)

Such texts will need excellent readers and perhaps brief com-
ments to help us hear their words. The reference in the final lines of
the Saturday homily to the bridal dwelling chamber, for example, is
echoed in the Exsultet and various blessings of water. It seems a
primary image in the church's keeping of these days. A fifth-century
bishop's homily reads: "Never was earth adorned with a tomb
which sheltered real life, or rather by a tomb which proved to be a
wedding chamber!" Yet most of us are far from living with such
images, though their basis still is real for us, the marriage bed and
the tomb. It is this richness to these days that we lack when
resurrection is reduced to a dead body coming back to life.

The presence of these ancient homilies should point us also
toward contemporary texts (the homilies of Bishop Oscar Romero,
for example) that speak from the scriptures to our lives. Take care
that we are not satisfied with anything too sweet, anything too
comforting. There is comfort and there is comfort.

Texts from the Office of Readings or from contemporary sources can be inserted to any of the hours that are prayed in the parish if this is done with a good sense for the flow of the whole prayer. Other traditions, such as the texts from Lamentations that were part of the Tenebrae liturgy, could well become part of the parish's tradition for prayer during the Triduum. Some of the more dramatic aspects of Tenebrae (e.g., the extinguishing of the candles one by one) are probably best not retained.

In the preparation of these rites, those responsible may find that they also could put together a simple handout (to be given on Palm Sunday) with home prayers for mornings and nights on these days. (See also the list of resources in the appendix, part 4.)

Generally, the presider and cantor should take their places in the circle or in the choir-style seating some time before the scheduled beginning of Morning Prayer or of any of the hours. With their example, the gathering will be in silence. Postures also are shown by example, without spoken directions. Normally, the group would stand at the beginning and the conclusion, sit for the psalms and readings, kneel for prayers of intercession. The conclusion also will be with the leaders simply remaining in place to continue their prayer and reflection. So that people may recognize the conclusion, one of the leaders should depart when the prayer is concluded.

Third Priority: Other Devotions

Holy Thursday: Devotions before the Blessed Sacrament. The sacramentary notes that "the faithful should be encouraged to continue adoration before the Blessed Sacrament for a suitable period of time during the night" but not beyond midnight. Night Prayer and the ongoing vigil would not take place in the chapel with the reserved sacrament but in the church.

The 1988 *Circular Letter* makes a suggestion from the church's tradition: Those keeping watch this night may wish to read from John's gospel, chapters 13 to 17, Jesus' final discourse. A good translation should be selected (e.g., the *New Revised Standard Version*) and the passages suitably divided. These could be read aloud, with a reading every five or ten minutes, or they could be prepared on suitable pages and made available to all who stay to pray. No other elaboration of this devotion before the Blessed Sacrament is needed.

Good Friday: Stations of the Cross. There are two possible situations: a parish where the stations are a familiar and well-attended devotion during Lent and on Good Friday, and parishes where this has not been the case. In the former, the parish probably has a format for stations that is expected by those who come. This may need work, both from the viewpoint of the texts (many, many versions of the stations are published; study especially those that make clear and consistent use of the scriptures) and the ritual (stations can become as audience-oriented as any other form of our prayer). Those for whom the stations are important should be consulted and involved.

In the latter case, where the stations have not recently been a popular form of devotion, initiating stations of the cross would not be a priority if the central liturgies of the Triduum and the liturgy of the hours are being emphasized. Like many devotional practices, the stations grew in popularity when much of the church's liturgy was not accessible to ordinary Catholics. The stations retain their attraction for some and this should be honored, but it should not take attention or effort away from the principal liturgies. (See the following notes in "Ecumenical Services" on the public way of the cross.)

Today, some ethnic and parish traditions include a form of the passion play. The gospel accounts of the arrest, trial, torture and execution of Jesus are a continuing source of dramatic expression for professionals and amateurs. In some ways, these plays are a means of evangelization. They allow a manifestation of faith that apparently is not yet possible in the liturgical celebrations. But today, as through many centuries, such dramas tend to have one failing that must be corrected: They frequently portray the Jewish people as the villains, the "Christ-killers." They do not, perhaps they cannot, give the total picture: the hated and brutal Roman occupation, the many sides of Jewish resistance and the side of Jewish collaboration, Jesus as a Jew who was close to the Pharisees in his teaching and much more.

Passion plays tend to proclaim a "bad Jews versus good Jesus" story, often with the Roman Pilate as the would-be friend of Jesus or as a bumbling governor. Certainly, this is not all such dramas are about. Especially in the Mexican-American community, they manifest the identification of an oppressed people with a suffering Jesus. In such communities, the plays are likely to represent an important effort among members of various parishes to give public witness to their faith. Such things might well be continued even while—in the script and manner of portrayal—giving attention to the church guidelines that warn against the mistakes often made in dramatizing the passion. Those responsible should be thoroughly familiar with the guidelines published by the United States bishops: *Criteria for the Evaluation of Dramatizations of the Passion* (USCC Publishing Services). Even when every effort is made here, parishes have to be careful that the dramatic production doesn't cut deeply into the energy needed for liturgy.

Good Friday: Three Hours Devotion. Some parishes have retained or initiated a form of the Three Hours devotion from noon until three o'clock, leading then into the principal liturgy of Good Friday. Such a ritual might begin with Midday Prayer from the liturgy of the hours and might expand to be the type of vigiling prayer (scripture and other reading, long periods of silence, psalmody and ostinati, occasional hymns) that will happen at the Easter Vigil itself. This would have an informal character, allowing people to come and go as they wish. If stations of the cross are traditional, they could be incorporated within this service but not in close proximity to the liturgy that follows. If the day's principle liturgy does not begin at three o'clock, the Three Hours devotion could conclude with Midafternoon Prayer from the liturgy of the hours.

Good Friday: Ecumenical Services. In these years, the Roman Catholic contribution to ecumenical services on Good Friday will come from our emerging sense for the Triduum itself and for these days as times of prayer and fasting that culminate in the Vigil. This is increasingly the tradition of some Lutherans, Episcopalians, Methodists and Presbyterians, but it will not be the tradition of many others. Today, we still have few occasions that bring us together to pray. Catholics can offer what is essential in our sense for Good

Friday, that binding of glory and cross that we read in John's gospel and sing in the "Vexilla Regis" and some other chants and hymns. The veneration of a cross within such a liturgy may add a dimension of gesture that otherwise would be entirely missing.

Some ecumenical services take the form of a way of the cross that visits places where the practice of the gospel is tested today: jails and prisons, schools, homes for the elderly, hospitals, places where there has been discrimination based on race or sex or any other factor, places that remind us to protest against poor treatment of the environment, against weapons and pornography—these are places to stop and pray and read the scriptures. Every urban community can identify such a way of the cross. The need is for texts, scriptural and contemporary, that speak briefly and with conviction, and for songs that can be sung by everyone when moving from place to place. Such services are not meant to be lectures but rituals, and great care must be taken to protect this.

The Blessing of Easter Foods. In many traditions, it is customary to bless the foods that will break the fast on Easter. Special breads, produce, eggs and meat are brought to the church to be blessed. These are the foods not eaten during Lent. When the Easter Vigil was on Saturday morning—as it was for centuries—and the lenten fast ended at noon on Saturday, the timing of the blessing was right. Now the timing is a problem. But only the timing: Wherever possible, the tradition of binding home and community through this blessing should be strengthened, and it could well be introduced where it is not yet known.

Parishes that have moved these blessings to the liturgies of Easter, beginning with the Vigil, have had great success. Some have set a special time for the blessings, keeping them apart from the Mass only because of the lack of space for the food. Texts for the Easter blessing of foods are found in the *Book of Blessings,* chapter 54, but many communities will have other texts from their traditions. If the parish is to make something of this, then the various foods should be blessed one at a time, not all at once. Eggs are blessed as eggs, meat as meat, bread as bread. Each has its individual way of proclaiming the festival of the resurrection.

Catechetical Assemblies for Children. Often the principal liturgies of these days will not attract parents with young children because of the length and the time of day. The parish should make great efforts to provide child care during these services or perhaps to offer home baby-sitting on Thursday and Saturday nights; the problem is where to find the baby-sitters if we want everyone possible at the liturgy. That is a problem that can be solved.

In the 1992 *Sourcebook for Sundays and Seasons,* Thomas Ryan suggests that in many parishes, the children of primary and intermediate grades could be offered a time to assemble on Good Friday and Holy Saturday mornings:

> They would gather each day for an hour-long event organized more or less as a celebration of the word. What distinguishes this from being a "children's liturgy" competing with the principal liturgy is that it must clearly point to the parish assembly—a kind of rehearsal and preparation to enable children to participate fully in the principal liturgies. On Good Friday morning, such an assembly may include:
>
> — Music that opens the experience of the passion and the cross and that also will be used at the Celebration of the Lord's Passion.
>
> — A reading or two from the day's liturgy of the hours, using images with which children can identify.
>
> — Instructions, given by one or more of the parish leaders, that introduce the liturgy that they will enter later in the day, helping everyone enter its image-world. Instructions may be given in smaller groups by age level.
>
> — Rehearsal and gracious explanations for the solemn actions that they will perform with the adults later on. Such rehearsals are like a preparatory act of prayer.
>
> — Some preparation of the physical requirements of the principal liturgy: For example, children can see the stripped-down church and reflect on it, or help to prepare a resting place for the cross, or get the cross out of storage and bring it to the place from which it will be carried in solemn entrance.
>
> — Praying some of the general intercessions chosen from the Celebration of the Lord's Passion.

Further Possibilities

The Holy Saturday session could include:

— The participation of the children in the preparation of the elect, especially if children of catechetical age will be initiated.

— The participation of the children in the parish Morning Prayer or Midday Prayer; if the children will be present in large numbers, those who prepare the liturgy could select psalms and prayers that facilitate the children's entrance into this prayer.

— The painting of Easter eggs to be blessed and distributed to all after the Vigil and on Sunday.

— Hearing (and dramatizing) scriptures of the Vigil.

— Preparing the worship space for the great night.

One great task of these gatherings is the teaching of silence. A deliberate silence should be woven through all these efforts.

Holy Saturday: Approaching the Vigil. The Easter Vigil always is to begin after it is dark. It is to end before daybreak of Sunday. Relatively few parishes have chosen midnight or later to begin this liturgy. Most begin around eight o'clock (but this depends on the date of Easter and whether daylight saving time is in effect).

The concern here is twofold. First, the Vigil—like the other liturgies of the Triduum—is related to what has gone before and what follows. It does not "begin," it "continues." How is that to be seen in the parish? Can the Vigil be clearly in continuity with the fasting and prayer and watching that began on Thursday night and have continued until now?

Second, the Vigil as we have it now contains only a portion of those scriptures that have been part of it in the past.

The suggestion is that without creating another ritual, the parish's Triduum intensify somewhat late on Saturday afternoon, simply by having the quiet reading of various scriptures. These would be texts that once were part of the Vigil or now are part of the Vigil in other churches. Anyone, baptized or elect, would be welcome to join in listening to these scriptures and quietly reflecting on them. There is no opening and no closing; people are free to come and go as they wish. There would be no presider, just an order of the readers. The group would be small enough to gather together and not use microphones. A cantor could introduce psalmody in some spots, using psalms that will be sung later in the night. This time of reading, of building toward the Vigil itself, could continue as darkness falls, then fade into the Vigil liturgy.

The following are readings that have had some association with the Vigil that are not now in the Roman lectionary for this night:

Genesis 5–9 (selections; the story of Noah)

Ezekiel 37:1–14 (the dry bones)

Isaiah 4:1–6; 5:1–2 (the Lord's glory, our shelter and shade)

Jonah (the entire story)

Deuteronomy 31:19–30; 32:1–4, 7, 36, 43 (the song of Moses)

Daniel 3:1–56 (the three young men in the fiery furnace)

Zephaniah 3:8–20 (the Lord gathering the remnant)

Isaiah 61:1—62:5 (you shall no more be forsaken)

2 Kings 4:8–37 (Elisha and the Shunammite woman)

Isaiah 63:11—64:5 (tear open the heavens and come down)

The Vigil

Where did a night like this come from? And can it, at the end of the twentieth century, mean churches filled with people for hours and hours on this Saturday night/Sunday morning?

It did not come solely from a need to celebrate the death and the resurrection of the Lord, for that was done each Sunday. This yearly Passover of the church certainly has its roots in Jewish Christians who continued to celebrate Passover, but this annual celebration of Israel's passover and of Jesus' passover eventually drew to itself the community's need to climax the long initiation process for new members of the church. Around these catechumens, the already baptized renewed their own life-and-death experience.

Lent grew as a formalization of the last days before baptism, the homestretch, and became a time when the baptized who had wandered could return to the church. This night then was—for one amazing period in the church's life—a vigil crowned with baptism and anointing and eucharist. The 50 days that followed were the overflowing of this.

No one could ignore it any more than a child could ignore the preparation for, birth of and room-around-the-table for a new member in the family. The late winter and early spring months brought the approach to the font, the baptism bath in water, the fragrant oil, the bread and the wine at our welcome table.

For better or worse, the church has in this century set itself to renew that experience. This is not at all a romantic attachment to some ideal days of the past. It is more a hardheaded recognition—a shocking recognition perhaps, given some of our history—that baptism makes the church and the church had better keep its heart and eye and mind fixed on those waters. This is in part the way things work in the world: The way a tribe initiates its young or its newcomers is forever the way that that tribe defines its own existence. But for us, there is more. It may seem sometimes that this church is a little like a club we belong to, or a support group, or a crutch to lean on in difficult times or a cranky but still lovable bit of nostalgia. But once we let baptism into the picture, no more!

The following two sections, taken from *An Introduction to Lent and Eastertime* (LTP), attempt to help us remember and understand this. (See also Aidan Kavanagh's account of the Vigil night in the appendix, part 1.)

The only place we can begin is in the dark, the dark of a Saturday night and Sunday morning. People are quietly assembling. They may be many or few. They come as individuals, couples, households, friends. Some of them are light-headed from 48 hours of a strict fast; they are hungry to be in this assembly tonight. In the darkness outside, a bonfire is burning and from it a great candle is lighted. All move inside and by the light of that candle a member of the assembly sings a summons to rejoicing: Angels, earth, church, everyone here: Rejoice! The singer proclaims that this is our passover, that this— tonight, if you would believe it—is the night when the slaves were delivered to freedom and safety, the night when God raised up Jesus and broke death's hold on us. This night (the song continues) will see evil driven away, the proud humbled, mourners rejoicing, hatred take flight and peace settle in.

Then for a long time in the darkness, the assembled people listen to what perhaps are their most sacred scriptures. On this one night of all the year, the book is opened to its first page. Only on this night do the people hear the wonderful and amazing words that are written on that page: "In the beginning . . ." Over and over again come the words that both judge and direct everyday life: "God saw how good it was!" And when that page has been read and pondered, readers turn to the story of God's promise to Abraham; to the story of how the slaves escaped right through the sea; to the poems of Isaiah where God woos a people "afflicted, storm-battered and unconsoled," and where the penniless are summoned to feast in a

The Vigil:
What We Do

realm where the tables are turned; to Baruch's summons to search our God's ways for "she has appeared on earth and moved among us"; to Ezekiel's promise of a new heart; to Paul's dazzling and right question: "Are you not aware that we who were baptized in Christ Jesus were baptized into his death?" *(into his death?)*; and last, to the page of the gospel that tells the story of the empty tomb.

When all of these scriptures have been heard with silences and psalms between them, a chant begins. The singer calls out the names of the ancestors; saints of all times and places are summoned now to stand with this generation, to stand around a font full of water. Here, beside the waters, the elect (who were chosen 40 days ago and told to make final preparations to do battle with evil and fix their hearts on good, to pray and fast so as to come ready this night) are left in no doubt about the stakes. They are asked to make renunciations, asked to say publicly that they will turn away from an entire way of life. One by one they do this, then profess eagerly that which will bind them to this people: a life lived by faith in God who is Creator and Redeemer and Holy Spirit.

Then each one enters the pool of water and is baptized, poured over or dipped three times. The point is drowning. The point, quite simply, is death. For to be baptized in Christ is to be "dead and have one's life hid with Christ in God" (Paul to the Colossians 3:3). All this really has not changed since it was described 1,600 years ago:

> The ones being baptized truly die by a symbol of that death by which the life-giver of all died; and they surely live with a type of life without end. Sin and death they put off and cast away in baptism, after the manner of those garments which our Lord departing left in the tomb. As a babe from the midst of the womb they look forth from the water; and instead of garments the priest receives them and embraces them. They resemble babes when they are lifted from the midst of the water and as babes everyone embraces and kisses them. Instead of swaddling clothes they cast garments on their limbs, and adorn them as brides and grooms on the day of the marriage supper.

After the waters comes the perfumed oil called chrism, poured on each newly baptized head, sealing the baptism as the sweet odor fills the hall. Then all join in making intercession to God for the world's needs. Bread and wine are brought to the holy table where with prayer and acclamation they are blessed; after sharing the kiss of peace, all eat of the one bread and drink from the one cup. All alike are members of Christ whose body and blood are their nourishment, peace and bond.

What we do this night is, to all appearances, very strange, very unworldly. What can it have to do with the stuff of daily lives or the passions and deeds that claim the world's attention? Here we are, sitting in the dark for long readings, none of which came into being any less than 1,900 years ago. We are speaking strange, even foreign words: words such as *renounce* and *alleluia* and *body and blood*. We are gathered around a small pool of ordinary water where we immerse or splash the newcomers, then acclaim them, embrace them and anoint them with oil.

What Kind of Deeds Are These?

Who in the world would give up a Saturday night for this?

Yet for those who gather, this is the most worldly Saturday night of the year. It is the night of all nights most about this world. The life that is affirmed and embraced this night is not merely some afterlife of bliss. The death that we proclaim defeated is not merely the death that each of us must die. This is the most worldly of nights because what is defeated—so we hear and so we mean, though the news is traveling slowly—is death in life, that death that masquerades as life: the death that dwells in economic and political systems when any human being is without food or dignity, the death that dwells in our very selves when we live at ease with bounty and allow the balance to grow more and more lopsided while we continue beating our children's plowshares into a sword. Defeated is that death that dwells in homes and nations when we learn and teach that any color is better, any sex, any age, any nationality, any status.

This night we affirm the death of all that death, for we know— just hear those scriptures, just look at that woman entering the waters, just smell that chrism, just taste that cup—what is passing away and what abides. This is our passover, that paschal mystery that we proclaim: Dying Christ destroyed our death, rising Christ restored our life. The liturgy this night is worldly through and through, just as we are and will be. It is ours. It is what we need, what we undoubtedly cannot do without if we desire the making of new Christians and the renewing of old Christians.

It is clear that no one gets up from the dinner table on this Saturday night and strolls over to the church for such a Vigil. Nor does anyone walk out afterward expecting a typical Sunday. The Vigil can exist only within its own time, the Triduum, and the Triduum prepared by Lent and overflowing into Eastertime.

Images of This Night

Those who prepare the liturgy and minister at the liturgy of the Vigil begin not with the lists of details but with reflection and discussion about the understanding of this night that has been given here. They also can take time to know this night through its verbs. The action words for what we are doing can keep us straight amid the details. Here is one list, a starter.

> Hush . . .   Shiver . . . Ignite . . . Flicker . . . Blaze . . . Light up . . . Warm up . . . Smell . . . Follow . . . Acclaim . . . Read and read and read . . . Listen and listen and listen . . . Sing and sing and sing . . . Ask . . . Stand . . . Invoke . . . Splash . . . Flow . . . Breathe . . . Mingle . . . Dip . . . Bring forward . . . Renounce and denounce . . . Swear and promise . . . Drown . . . Emerge . . . Acclaim . . . Clothe . . . Surround . . . Embrace . . . Anoint . . . Petition . . . Prepare . . . Invite . . . Gather . . . Bless . . . Break . . . Pour . . . Share . . . Go.

With lectionary and sacramentary in hand, one can make a list of lively nouns twice as long. It is best not to review the past year's order of service or its evaluation until through some reading and exercises those responsible have again thoroughly remembered what the Vigil is intended to be.

The liturgy of this night is to the year what Sunday is to the week. Everything goes toward it; everything comes from it. Yet nothing is more obvious than the futility of trying to realize such a Vigil by simply pouring immense efforts into the night's details. The Vigil cannot do its task unless it is the summit *of something,* unless it is the source *of something.* We only have to look at this liturgy to know that it is the work of a people who cling to and treasure scripture (at home, in assembly), a people who are disciplined (and frustrated) by a kind of fasting that gives them clarity and perspective, a people who are humble before their oldest members and their newest members, a people who want (but little by little usually) to stake everything on "alleluia" being the final word (rather than, for example, "What we say goes" or "Buy low, sell high" or "That's mine"). So liturgy doesn't sit in its corner and plan a grand Vigil. It can't be done.

What can be done is this: If this church is facing up to its baptism, even though it fails and knows it more often than not, then let's go to this night and do it as best we can. Let's do it as hungry as we can stand it, a fire that's a fire, scripture that sounds like great poetry and stories we could listen to all night long, baptizing that looks like somebody took on death and was embraced by the living God, chrism that makes the whole place smell unbelievably good and a table that still has that poor bread and little sip of the cup for which we are so hungry and thirsty.

We begin now by looking briefly at the main lines and concerns in each part of the Vigil. Those who prepare must clearly understand the whole liturgy, its order and the relationships, before getting down to details. Then we discuss the room and the ministries and the practical needs. Finally, we look at each part of the Vigil in detail.

Tonight, the liturgy does not begin with the kind of Sunday entrance rite that must take us from various worlds into community so that we can hear the word and do the eucharist. Tonight, the liturgy assumes that we are gathered: We've been here two days now!

The Gathering: An Overview

After dark—and darkness is essential, as the documents emphasize again and again—those who have regathered assemble outside and do the sensible thing: Light a fire. Christians have been starting their late evening prayer that way for centuries, always with praise to Christ who is our light. But this night, coming after the 40 days of Lent and the 48 hours of fasting and praying, isn't satisfied with a small candle or small fire. This is a once-a-year fire. This is the fire that starts all fire over again. It is lighted, blazes away, is blessed and is used to light the great candle that this church will hold and treasure through the coming year. A procession forms, led by that candle, and enters the dark church. Now there is the rich smell of incense. Handfuls have been thrown on the fire, and from the fire hot coals have been taken and put into thuribles and covered with incense.

When all have come into the room, one of the ministers stands in the light of the candle and sings the Exsultet, a eucharistic prayer of blessing God over the people, the candle, the night. The poetry of this song resonates through all that is to follow.

The Scriptures: An Overview

The sacramentary calls the liturgy of the word "the fundamental element of the Easter Vigil." "Fundamental"—as in "that on which everything else is built," as in "that without which everything else isn't going to stand or make sense."

At present, there are nine readings. The sacramentary allows that number to be reduced, but then what becomes of this "fundamental element"? If we include only four or six or eight readings, we chip away at the foundation. We chip away at that which supports absolutely everything else that we do this night.

One problem is the attitude that this Vigil is just a Sunday Mass with a few things thrown in. Another is the attitude that presumes people just won't put up with being here for more than two hours. The first is wrong on the face of it: This is a vigil—and while we may not know much about vigils, we do know that they are something one hunkers down for. That's the point.

The second attitude—that people won't put up with a three- or four-hour liturgy—has been shown to be wrong again and again and again in the past decade. In cities and suburbs and in rural areas are parishes where the Vigil lasts that long and people come early and stay late. They are not exceptional people, not professional Catholics. They are people in parishes where the care and attention to the dialogue of liturgy and life has had great priority. There are, in fact, parishes where the number of readings has been extended to include some of the texts not in the present lectionary, such as the Noah story and the Song of Songs, that are of great importance to this night.

All through the Triduum, and especially tonight, convenience and concerns about time have no place. If the length is a problem for some people, they will choose not to attend next year. When the liturgy is as it should be, though, time will practically vanish as a factor. People will look at their watches afterward and not believe how many hours have passed. We easily fall into a way of thinking that makes decisions based on the lowest common denominator. Liturgy never was intended to be about doing things in a way that people believe will please them.

So through all the readings there is a rhythm of listening and quiet reflection, the latter often aided by psalmody, leading to a prayer.

The essence of this time is this: Here is the end of our fasting; these words, these scriptures are what we needed to grow hungry for. On a full stomach, it would be hard to know how much each one needs to hear "In the beginning . . ." and "Take your child, your only child . . ." and "This is like the days of Noah for me." And on and on. We learn what we are hungry for here. Hungry to hear these pages read, hungry to sing our songs, keep some silence, join in prayer. It is all right to doze off for a while, all right to get up and stretch, all right to walk outside. This can even be communicated to people in an invitational comment at the beginning of the liturgy of the word.

This is our house; that's our book; we need time together. For a wonderful image of the liturgy of the word tonight, see Brian Helge's introduction to the readings in *Triduum Sourcebook* (LTP), page 77. He says in part:

> Tonight we are going to tell our name—to ourselves, by way of reminder, to those who will become part of us this night through baptism and confirmation, and to those of the world who will listen. And our name is a very long one, one that has been growing since the creation of the world. . . . None of us would be here if we did not think that the name was worth telling and listening to. Now the trick of this kind of name telling is to relax. You cannot be hasty in this time ahead of us. Haste will stop up your ears finally, and then you will not hear this lovely language and our beautiful name. Relax and make yourself comfortable in the darkness and don't even try to "make sense" of the name. Just hear it, let it roll over you in waves of meaning.

There is one of the basic observations about liturgy, not just in this liturgy of the word and not just in this Vigil, but always: "Haste will stop up your ears." Do we believe that? Certainly, we have experienced it. A good pace by itself, of course, will get us nowhere tonight. The words that are read must come from lectors who have been amazed by these words once again and know how to give us that same amazement.

Near the end of the readings, the pace quickens a bit. Then the Alleluia returns from its lenten exile so that we can acclaim the single reading from the gospel. The homily is difficult to fix: It should presume that we have been listening long and hard and we now want to get on with the baptisms. But it is the one time when all that we do tonight can explicitly become the measure of our world and times. So it is not necessarily that short, though every word is packed.

When this "fundamental element" is done well, then we have something to build on.

Baptism, Anointing and Eucharist: An Overview

Following the homily, the church calls on the saints, all those who have walked in this way before, to process with us now to the font. A deacon or acolyte carries the Easter candle at the head of the procession, followed by the elect and their godparents, then the presider and other ministers. When the font is in a space apart from the main area of the church, the whole assembly joins in the procession, perhaps following the candle and leading the elect and the ministers.

Before or after the procession, the elect are called and presented by their godparents. At the font, God is blessed over the waters in the words sung by the presider and acclaimed by the assembly. Then the elect come forward to renounce sin and profess their faith, and immediately are led into the waters of the font and are baptized. Each baptism is acclaimed in song by the assembly. Then the whole assembly renews the renunciations and professions of baptism, and the baptismal water is sprinkled generously on the whole assembly.

Anyone who has been previously baptized and has been prepared for reception into full communion with the Catholic church

is called forward to complete the baptismal promises with a profession of faith. This is acknowledged by the presider. The newly baptized and newly received then are anointed with chrism in confirmation.

For the first time, the neophytes take part in the general intercessions and in the eucharistic prayer. For the first time, they join the faithful in the kiss of peace and the procession to holy communion where, to quote the story from Aidan Kavanagh (in the appendix, part 1): "They dine on the precious Body whose true and undoubted members they have become, drink the precious Blood of him in whom they themselves have now died."

A Sense for the Order

This overview is intended for those who prepare the liturgy and those in the principal ministries. These people must have the flow of the gathering, the vigiling, the baptizing and the eucharist at their fingertips. Then some of them must get down to details.

In preparation for the liturgy, it helps to answer this question from a stranger: What is it that your people do on Holy Saturday night? This makes us reduce the previously discussed overview even further so that we can say something like:

> Well, we finished Lent on Holy Thursday evening and since then most people have been to church several times, but we pray and read scripture at home also—and we don't watch TV or go shopping or do any real work. And we don't eat, or we eat very little, from Thursday night on. So we're hungry when we come on Saturday night after it gets dark. We begin around a fire and carry candles inside, and for a long time we just listen to the Bible and sing: the creation story, Isaac, the Red Sea, the women finding the tomb empty and much more. Then everybody crowds around the baptism pool and we baptize all those who have been preparing for this through a year or longer. That is the real climax of the night. These people then are confirmed when a perfumed oil is poured over their heads; then they change into new clothes and go with us around the altar where we do what we always do: Lift up our hearts, give God thanks and praise, share the holy communion.

Once one has a sense for the basic integrity of the Vigil, when it no longer is just a list of ceremonies to cope with, then we can get down to the details.

The sacramentary has long said to have the Vigil in the dark. Disregard of that rubric was one thing that prompted the 1988 *Circular Letter*. No other single subject in the letter is given as much space as this matter of the time of the Vigil and the reasons for it. These paragraphs are quoted in their entirety here. The tone, especially in offering the rationale, is almost passionate on this matter.

The Time of the Vigil

> According to a most ancient tradition, this night is "one of vigil for the Lord" (Exodus 12:42), and the vigil celebrated during it to commemorate that holy night when the Lord rose from the dead is regarded as the "mother of all vigils" (Augustine). For in that night the church keeps vigil, waiting for the resurrection of the Lord, and celebrates the sacraments of Christian initiation.
>
> "The entire celebration of the Easter Vigil takes place at night. It should not begin before nightfall; it should end before daybreak on Sunday" (Sacramentary). This rule is to be taken according to its strictest sense. Reprehensible are those abuses and practices which have crept in many places in violation of this ruling, whereby the Easter Vigil is celebrated at the time of day that it is customary to celebrate anticipated Sunday Masses.
>
> Those reasons which have been advanced in some quarters for the anticipation of the Easter Vigil, such as lack of public order, are not put forward in connection with Christmas night nor other gatherings of various kinds. . . .
>
> From the very outset the church has celebrated that annual Pasch, which is the solemnity of solemnities, above all by the means of a night vigil. For the resurrection of Christ is the foundation of our faith and hope, and through baptism and confirmation we are inserted into the paschal mystery of Christ, dying, buried and raised with him, and with him we shall also reign.
>
> The full meaning of vigil is a waiting for the coming of the Lord. (#77–80)

The first thing to be said, then, is that there should be no doubt about the importance placed on the tiny rubric in the sacramentary about not starting "before nightfall." It matters greatly. Even worries about the safety of parishioners after dark are not to change this. (These are real worries in some parishes, and contrary to the document, worries about safety have caused the time of Christmas "Midnight" Mass to be changed or the Mass to be dropped. But the Easter Vigil is of another order altogether from the Christmas custom. That is exactly what the rest of the document's argumentation is about. What this should suggest to us is that part of organizing for the Vigil is organizing whatever is needed to make people feel safe in coming out at night. In more ways than this one, the Easter Vigil could adopt the slogan of many women's groups: Take back the night!)

The second thing to mark is that the document goes on to show why it matters that this liturgy be in the darkness of Saturday night to Sunday morning. The argument is as simple as the Exsultet: "This is the night," it sings over and over. The darkness is our bond with the deeds of liberation by which Jews and Christians were created and delivered to freedom and life. The document cheats a bit when it resorts to a "the church has always taught" attitude: "From the very outset the church has celebrated that annual Pasch . . . above all by the means of a night vigil." Yes, from somewhere near the outset there was a night vigil, but that was lost for many centuries before it was restored during the 1950s.

But what finally is remarkable about this passage is its ready linking of the sacraments of initiation to the night vigil. "For in that night the church keeps vigil . . . and celebrates the sacraments of Christian initiation." Also: "For the resurrection of Christ is the foundation of our faith and hope, and through baptism and confirmation we are inserted into the paschal mystery of Christ, dying, buried and raised with him." Perhaps this is a simple recognition of what has been for two decades in the sacramentary, but it comes as a strong endorsement for what is far from universal practice. It recognizes that this night is incomplete without the sacraments of initiation, but it seems to imply also—and we sometimes neglect this—that the sacraments need this night. "This is the night" is true and it is our deeds with water, chrism, bread and wine that make it so. But those deeds cannot achieve their full meaning at any other moment of our calendar.

The English translation previously used, "it should not begin before nightfall," seems to capture best what is intended. That is quite different from "should not begin until after sunset" or "sundown." "Nightfall" means what the prior sentence implies: "The entire celebration . . . takes place at night." For many parishes, that would imply rethinking their usual hour. In the United States, daylight saving time now begins the night between Saturday and Sunday in the first weekend of April. Thus Easter can come before or after the change in the clock. A parish cannot simply say, "The Vigil starts at 7:30 in the evening." It depends on the date. It usually is fairly easy to check in an almanac for the time of sunset on Saturday, then to set the hour for beginning the Vigil. "At night" and "nightfall" would imply at least an hour after sunset. But the Vigil does not have to start at the earliest possible hour. It can begin later, and some parishes have moved in this direction: The vigiling in church intensifies on Saturday late afternoon and evening, gathering more and more people until, perhaps at ten o'clock, all go outside where the fire is lighted.

Before deciding what efforts to make with the lighting during the Vigil, we need a context. Some would argue that those of us who live with ready access to light at every hour have lost the sense for what night is and so the sense for a night vigil, and that the great emphasis on doing this liturgy at night is pointless when we have not the same sense for night as our ancestors. They would argue that "let's pretend it's dark" approaches are merely theatrical because people in our society turn on the lights at night except to sleep. Why not simply turn on the lights, because we never can hope to have the same sense for darkness and for light-in-darkness that our ancestors had?

This is a serious concern. In some ways, it is similar to a concern for the way we continue to do the liturgy of the word: We open our book and we read. But that is not how people in this technological society communicate. Television is, primarily. And again, some argue that this generation's constant exposure to screens and their images has altered the very ability to relate to the simple spoken word. Yet we cling to our book and our reading. Is it sufficient to argue that this is basic human communication—a real mouth speaking to real ears, a live human addressing other live humans— and the only form that befits a church like ours? And, regarding the

Lighting

matter of night, can we argue that there is a power in darkness that is even stronger because darkness has become so foreign to us? Can we argue that, regardless of our access to lights at any hour, the rhythm set by darkness and light as they alternate continues to be in our minds and hearts?

All of this places the matter of the time of the Vigil back before us. Perhaps the essential thing we are after is not only darkness but also the part of the night that finds people in bed. Our easy ability to keep plenty of light around us is mostly what we do in the evening. The Vigil must be a night when we do what we ordinarily do not do. In part, yes, that is simply not using the light that is accessible to us. But in larger part, it may be that what the Vigil asks is being there when we usually would be doing the normal thing of night, sleeping. Instead, we are here and we are keeping watch. The vigiling/watching that was dimly sensed in Lent and since Thursday night has filled us with eagerness, now is in its final hours. This is the rehearsal of all of life and all of being the church, for it is looking for the reign of God that we touch in this Passover night.

The argument about lighting then may be a matter of saying: When general light is not needed in the room, we will not use it because its absence is striking, out of the ordinary for our assembly, and that goes with everything else about this Vigil. Its absence, in fact, lets the night be night, and doesn't interfere. And for a people unused to being awake in the darkness, that may not be exactly what it was for earlier generations, but it does not seem out of harmony with what got them to keep vigil and, for centuries, kept them gathering in the darkness.

That said, it must be added that the lights are not to be turned into theater. The whole liturgy should be considered and carefully marked for the person who takes charge of the lighting. Gathering outside and going into the church, the light comes from the fire and the candles. Only dim safety lights (near stairs, for example) should be on; if the people carry candles and if these candles will be lighted before they enter the church, then no other lights should be needed and all the interior lights should not be turned on. If the people enter the church with unlighted candles, perhaps some single, very low light in the nave of the church is lighted, and even that can be only for safety during the time people must find chairs or pews. For the singing of the Exsultet, ministers with lighted candles should surround the singer (who stands anyway in the light of the Easter candle).

Likewise, the light for the readers can come from candelabra placed beside the book. This also may be adequate for the cantor. Whatever artificial light is needed for the choir should be used; it is not theatrics to raise this light only as needed during the psalmody. An acolyte with a candle accompanies the acolyte with the book when the presider is to lead the prayers after each reading. We are, in all this, keeping the use of light functional and not general. Yes, we could make this place bright as ever, but we must strike tonight on both ancient and contemporary ways that we humans relate to and in darkness.

The usual practice, in those parishes that make the effort to keep darkness through the readings from Hebrew Scriptures, has been to bring up, gradually or at once, all the light at the Gloria or the Alleluia. Why? It seems that we still are looking for "the moment" of the resurrection. One could argue against any great change in the lighting here. Acolytes with candles naturally accompany the gospel procession. Then, after the homily, all the candles the assembly holds can be lighted as we sing the litany and go toward the font, and the candles can remain lighted as long as people wish (in the Orthodox church, those attending will have two or three or more small candles for the four- or five-hour liturgy so that as one burns down another can be lighted). This depends, of course, on the assembly not needing to handle hymnals or missalettes or even the handout. It depends on staying faithful to the elements of the ritual so that we sing only litanies and refrains and acclamations, things we already know by heart or learn in the night's repetition. Normally, the people put their candles out at the sprinkling. Perhaps that is the time when adequate but not abundant artificial lighting is used and kept on through the dismissal.

Questions of candles and lighting should not be resolved apart from some reflection on all the ancient understandings of baptism as illumination, as enlightenment. These do not have to be seen as goodness/light versus evil/dark worldviews. At some first level, they simply express a human gratitude for light that implies the worth of the darkness also.

Preparing the Space

The Vigil does not call for lavishness. The starkness of the preceding hours of the Triduum prevails. If possible, Eastertime banners and even flowers should be held back for Sunday morning—although this means that some people will be up all night. This allows those responsible to continue to fast from their work until after the Vigil (and there is the custom in some places of bringing flowers into the space during the liturgy itself, perhaps as part of the return of the Alleluia to the church as the gospel procession begins). Even when banners and other things must be put in place on Holy Saturday afternoon, the work can be done in a retreatlike manner.

The Vigil is filled with things that are essential: fire, candle, book, water, towels, garments, chrism, bread and wine, vesture. Every attention should go toward these. As for other additions to the environment, less will be more tonight. We have 50 days of Eastertime to let these things spill over into a space made festive with flowers and textiles.

The "house of the church" then might not look much different when the Vigil begins than it did during the time from the Friday liturgy until now. The altar still is bare. There is absolutely no excess furniture, candle holders, whatever. The holder for the Easter candle has been put in place. Water has been put in the font (but not in any holy water fonts as yet) and a vessel for pouring is nearby. The fire is built; the candle is ready. Books for the ministers were completed well before rehearsals and are in place. The chrism was taken to its place on Thursday and is ready. Fresh-baked bread is ready at the last minute, and a wine (perhaps a variety used only at Easter) is in the refrigerator.

Outside there is the building of the fire. Sometimes this can be given to the Scouts (boy and girl) or to some other parish group and they can develop a tradition for preparing a large but safe fire, and a tradition for providing all the safeguards needed in case of wind or other troubles. They also would provide the alternative small fire for inside in case of a rainstorm or strong winds. The wood should be kept warm and dry to assure a good fire. And they would see the fire safely through without extinguishing it when the procession goes inside. If possible, the fire is still burning a little when people leave.

This night has its smells: the fire, many burning candles, plenty of incense (again, there are so many fine incenses now available; find one that will be used only for tonight and Eastertime), perhaps flowers. More subtle, but also possible, are the scents of the fresh bread and of the wine. The primary fragrance of this night, though, is chrism. Chrism is a mixture of vegetable oil (usually olive oil) and perfume (often, but not necessarily, a scent made from balsam). This mixture is made at the cathedral before the consecration of the chrism. Increasingly, those responsible are seeing to it that the chrism is truly fragrant. If this is not done, a small amount of perfume can be added in the parish, but this should be a scent especially prepared to mix with the oil. (Liturgy Training Publications, as well as other suppliers, carries such a fragrance prepared by Maria Arctander.) If the room is large, only a small number of people may smell the chrism, even if it is poured lavishly, unless some provision is made to bring people close to the newly baptized and anointed members of the church.

Rather than a tiny bottle, the chrism should have a fine container with a stopper and an equally fine pitcher (to pour over those being confirmed). If these are of glass, then the chrism can be seen.

The Fragrance of This Night

The Easter candle should be large enough and beautiful enough to be a sign of all that we name when the presider says:

> Christ yesterday and today,
> the beginning and the end,
> Alpha and Omega.
> All time belongs to him
> and all the ages.
> To him be glory and power
> through every age for ever. Amen.

The Easter Candle and Other Candles

The *Circular Letter* says of the candle:

> An Easter candle is prepared that can be a genuine sign that Christ is the light of the world: as such it should be made of wax—not of some synthetic material; it should be new each year, and should be of conspicuous size. The candle is blessed by using the signs and words indicated in the Missal or others approved by the conference of bishops. (#82)

Companies that sell candles now are likely to have Easter candles available in greater heights and widths than in the past. Sometimes these must be specially requested and ordered early. Very few offer anything of artistic value on the candle. Some parishes order a candle without any ornament; artists in the parish prepare wax ornamentation in appropriate colors. A parish's stand for the paschal candle may have to be replaced when the decision is made to use a larger candle because of the width and the weight of the candle. This may be an opportunity to have a craftsperson fashion a beautiful stand. This stand is one of the more visible pieces of furniture: present in the center of the assembly during the 50 days of Easter, present in the baptistry throughout the rest of the year and present at funerals beside the coffin.

Many parishes have members who are willing and able to make the candle themselves. There are various ways to do this (one of them is detailed in the appendix, part 8).

This is perhaps a good place to state the criteria for the parish's Easter candle—the same criteria that apply to all the objects used in liturgy. These are given in *Environment and Art in Catholic Worship* (Bishops' Committee on the Liturgy):

> To be true to itself and to protect its own integrity, liturgy must make demands. Basically, its demands are two: *quality* and *appropriateness*. . . . Quality means love and care in the making of something, honesty and genuineness with any materials used, and the artist's special gift in producing a harmonious whole, a well-crafted work. . . . The work of art must be appropriate in two ways: 1) It must be capable of bearing the weight of mystery, awe, reverence, and wonder which the liturgical action expresses; 2) it must clearly *serve* (and not interrupt)

ritual action which has its own structure, rhythm and movement. (#20–21)

Applied to the candle, these two criteria offer a more positive and broader evaluation than the cautions of the *Circular Letter.*

Perhaps all of the parish's old candles have been melted down to make the new Easter candle. Or at least they have been put aside, so that every candle in every candlestick, in every candelabra, and every candle carried by an acolyte tonight is a new candle, lighted for the first time from the one flame.

Some parishes, rather than provide the tiny candles for the assembly, now are inviting parishioners to bring new candles to the Vigil to be held lighted at the appropriate times and then to be burned in the home during the Easter season. An alternative would be to make fine candles for the homes available at the parish. Parishes can seldom afford to purchase and give away quality candles; they can, however, purchase good candles on consignment and offer them to parishioners at cost as their candles for the Vigil and for Eastertime. In any case, the candles given to the newly baptized should be of good size and quality.

In recent years, in many new churches and renovations, baptismal fonts for baptism by immersion have been built. "Immersion" is understood as that form of baptism where the adult can stand or kneel in a pool of water, perhaps waist deep but more often knee deep; water then is poured over the entire body of the person. In some cases, these pools also are used for baptism by submersion: The elect kneel in the water and the one who baptizes then takes hold of the head and shoulders and bends the person down until the whole body is under water. The one who baptizes also will, in most cases, enter the pool for baptizing an adult by immersion or submersion. Infants also are baptized in such pools or in elevated basins alongside the pool. Normally, an infant (except for the face) is submerged in the water.

These forms of baptism have been the preferred forms in all of the post–Vatican II revisions of the baptismal rites. Where such

The Font, Robes and Sprinkling the Assembly

fonts have been constructed, they usually make it possible for the assembly to gather around the font or to have a clear sight of it from their seating. (For numerous examples of such fonts, see *A Place for Baptism* by Regina Kuehn [LTP, 1992].) Where such a font exists, those who prepare the space must see that it is cleaned and ready before the Triduum, then filled before the Vigil. Flowers or other marks of honor should be planned for all of Eastertime.

What of parishes that have not yet been able to create a font that meets the present expectations of the rite? If there are no adults, children or infants to be baptized, then the water of the existing font—perhaps with much additional water for people to take home—would be blessed.

But if there are adults or children to be baptized, the best solution may be a temporary font. Temporary, however, would not mean for tonight only. It would mean a font to be with us throughout the Eastertime, until Pentecost. Its location probably will be dictated by the existing arrangement, but preference might go to the area where people enter the body of the church—provided those attending the Vigil can either gather there or at least see clearly. Sometimes another area, even one near the altar, will have to be chosen. A temporary font should, if at all possible, be somehow seen as an extension of the permanent font.

What is the nature of this temporary font? "Honesty" might be the best word. It should not distract from the rite itself, not call undue attention to itself, not invite ridicule. And it should be watertight and allow a person to enter it safely. Some parishes have used simple stock tanks purchased from farm-supply companies. They are honest. They mean water. They don't leak. There is nothing phony or ridiculous about them. They must be filled with a hose and emptied with a siphon, but the same is true of many of the permanent fonts that have been built; plumbing simply is not possible in many cases. Other parishes have been able to use small backyard pools, though there usually is a need to cover the pool itself or to surround it with a shell of more appropriate material. Yet other parishes have found a temporary solution in landscape pools purchased from a garden store. Again, such pools should be so prepared that they can be present throughout Eastertime; this means keeping the water fresh and clean.

The temperature of the water is of some concern. It is not out of place for buckets of hot water to be carried to the font and added to the water already there just before the blessing of the water.

Regarding baptismal garments, practices vary from parish to parish. In some places, the newly baptized go to a sacristy or other room to dry themselves and change to good clothes that are, in effect, their baptismal garments. (But where the parish makes ample use of chrism, pouring it over the heads of those to be confirmed, this change of garments should take place after the confirmation.) Other parishes clothe the newly baptized in alblike robes (most of the time these really are albs). The rite itself makes the baptismal garment optional, but there is great meaning for us in the scriptural image that we "have put on Christ," been clothed with Christ. That image would seem to call for a full garment. And perhaps the association with the alb is good, if people come to think of this vestment as simply the clothing of the baptized, put on again by the presider on Sunday when the eucharist is itself the work of baptized people.

As with the candle and the bread, it often is possible and has many good effects when parishioners or even the sponsors or godparents can make the baptismal garments. (See the appendix, part 9, for patterns.)

A few other items are needed near the font. An adequate stack of towels should be close by for drying and wrapping the newly baptized until they go out to change clothes. A pitcher or bucket is needed if water is to be poured; beware of anything that could easily break (the metal bucket is the type of simple, functional object that seems out of place only because we have not been used to letting the baptismal sign speak loudly).

Finally, if the assembly is to be sprinkled with water from the font, bowls and evergreen branches are needed. Some parishes send a person down each aisle with an assisting acolyte who holds a bowl filled with the baptismal water. Others have the presider go up and down each aisle. Buckets and branches aren't needed in those parishes that organize this moment in the liturgy like the adoration of the cross: All present come to the font, perhaps in several "streams," to place their hands in the water and make the sign of the cross or simply rub the water into their faces. This can be a wonderful and right procession just when a procession is needed.

Bread

Those parishes that do not yet bake their own altar bread may want to do this at least on the great festivals (as a way of initiating this for every Sunday). Experiment first with the chosen recipe (see the appendix, part 7, for one example) so that those responsible know well before Easter that they can produce a bread with good texture, one that is scored and easy to divide into pieces. The loaves are brought to the table by the newly baptized and are divided at the breaking of the bread.

The Service of Light

The remaining sections of this chapter are detailed notes on each portion of the liturgy.

The outline of the light service is simple:

- Gathering outside
- (Lighting and) blessing the fire
- (Marking of the Easter candle)
- The procession (and lighting of all candles)
- The Exsultet

Because it is dark, and the church itself should have only safety lights on as people assemble, ushers have an important task of extending a simple welcome and helping people. Some parishioners may come early and wish to sit inside until it is time to gather at the fire. Others may gather there from the beginning. The ministers would be on hand as early as 30 minutes before the liturgy is scheduled to begin. They can first sit somewhere in the darkness to recollect themselves. Then, 15 minutes before the liturgy, they should take their places around the fire. This is to help gather people, but more than anything it is to be sure that, inside and outside, there is no scurrying around attending to details in these moments. All should be in readiness well beforehand.

The sacramentary offers great freedom with the service of light to adapt to local possibilities. That should not be an invitation to move this service to another point in the liturgy where it is taken to somehow signify the resurrection. As noted previously, when we gather in the dark, we strike a fire or light a candle. This is the way the church has traditionally done Evening Prayer with the lucernarium service. Tonight's liturgy is simply a more elaborate, once-a-year version of this. It is not at all an effort to say, "Right now is the resurrection." If we understand the Triduum, we know there has not been that kind of separation or playacting the scriptural stories. We started Holy Thursday's liturgy singing about the resurrection; we praised the resurrection on Good Friday. So we are not tonight looking for "the moment."

We instead are moving from all the individual and occasionally communal ways of fasting and praying into the final hours of the Vigil. And it is night. And we *are* looking for the resurrection. Every gesture we make says that we are—and because of the wonderful multiplicity of these gestures, we begin to sense just how unimaginably grand this resurrection of Christ, ourselves, all creation is.

There is no comparing the mistake involved in diminishing the fire to a tiny, short blaze inside the church with that involved in diminishing baptism to a trickle of water over the forehead. But there is no reason to be satisfied with leaving this night's fire as just a suggestion of fire. We have time tonight to do things right. And we know it can't hurt to begin with a fire that lights up the night, warms up the assembly and proclaims the largeness of what we are here about. (A Chicago inner-city parish accumulates Christmas trees in a safe place, then builds its fire on a vacant lot near the church: a proclamation to the whole neighborhood.)

If this large approach is taken to the fire, then it might be burning as the assembly gathers. The liturgy once made much of striking the new fire from flint and stone, but that no longer is the case. Those responsible for the fire could begin with a small blaze an hour beforehand, letting the light be a summons to the assembly. Near to the time for beginning, they could build it up. Or the traditional way of striking the fire when all have assembled can be followed. Note that the sacramentary seems to prefer the first option: "A large fire is prepared in a suitable place outside the church." The rubrics never mention lighting the fire, presuming it already is burning. (Note that the sacramentary does provide for the unusual case of a parish unable to have a "large fire" outside; see note 13 in the Easter Vigil section of the sacramentary.)

The *Circular Letter* has one general remark about these opening moments that should be applied to the fire, and it has one strong sentence about the fire itself:

> The first part of the Vigil consists of actions and gestures that should be carried out at a measured pace and with such gravity that, with the help of introductory comments and the liturgical prayers, the faithful will correctly grasp the meaning of the rites.
>
> In a suitable place outside the church, if possible, a large pile of kindling is prepared for the igniting of the new fire, the flame of which can be seen truly to banish the darkness and light up the night. (#82)

The *Letter* is, wisely, less interested in having things explained than it is in having them done with a "fullness and nobility" that will itself communicate in ritual's own terms. As for the fire, the expectation is for lighting up the night!

No one who has witnessed these opening rites done well can doubt their beauty and power: to gather outside in chilly darkness, to see the creeping flames and finally a great fire lighting and warming a closely gathered assembly, to follow the great Easter candle, acclaiming it in song and spreading its light until the church is brought out of darkness by hundreds of tiny flames and then, by that light, to hear the Exsultet chanted fully and gladly.

And no one who has witnessed all this done badly can doubt it would have been better not to try at all: a feeble fire, lights turned off only for a few moments, an aluminum Easter candle shell with a spring-held candle inside; a response to "Light of Christ" that no one knows; the Exsultet recited or badly sung—or shortened to the point of missing it.

The direction is clear both pastorally and liturgically: This rite is not a major element in the Vigil, but like all introductory rites, it is

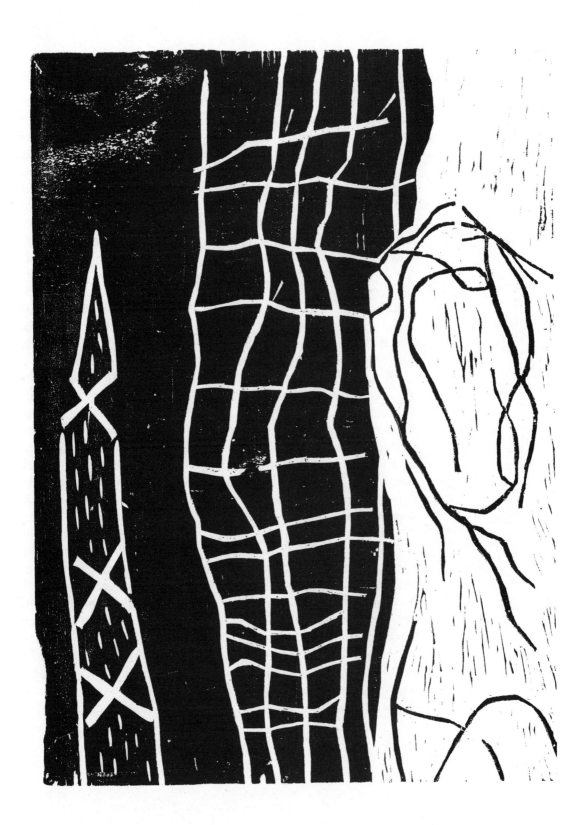

crucial. It gathers the community and it sets the tone. Only as much should be done as can be done well. No one should go home tonight remembering only the fire when they have joined in word and baptizing and eucharist. But, just as important, no one should go away uninvolved because nothing happened early on to get their attention, to pull the community together, to make them ready to hear and sing and baptize and do the eucharist.

The liturgy begins when those inside have been asked to come now around the fire and so have joined other parishioners, the elect and their godparents, the presider, perhaps a deacon, an assistant (probably a strong adult) holding the Easter candle, an acolyte with the service book, other acolytes with incense and thuribles (the pieces of charcoal are at the edge of the fire), other acolytes with unlighted candles, the cantor with the Exsultet book or scroll. The ushers are at the edges of the assembly, alert to any special needs. They have made sure that everyone has a candle.

Standing near the fire, the presider addresses the assembly with an announcement/invitation. The model given in the sacramentary is excellent, but this type of text is meant to be spoken directly. Reading it from a book weakens it. The presider, then, is to take from this text its thrust, its tone and its length, and with this to speak such an announcement to this assembly. Tone is important. This is not: "Well, how's everybody this evening?" It is formal because it comes from the last two days of fasting and prayer and it looks toward all the scripture and action that are ahead tonight.

This liturgy, like the gathering on Good Friday, does not begin with the sign of the cross and greeting. The presumption in both places is that the church already has (since Thursday night) been gathered and in prayer. All we do to begin these moments, then, is speak with some urgency and enthusiasm about where we now find ourselves.

Then the sacramentary (probably a worthy book that has been prepared especially to give order to the presider's texts alone) is brought forward and held in the light of the fire by one of the acolytes. The presider invites: "Let us pray." After a time of silence, the presider speaks loudly (above the sound of the fire) the opening prayer. Setting up a public-address system outside is not necessarily a good idea. Sometimes we should rely on the human voice. And there is no need to encourage any more words in this part of the liturgy.

The preparation of the candle is an optional part of the liturgy. The sacramentary suggests that a parish may have "other symbolic rites" that stress the significance of the Easter candle. Some parishes have chosen not to do the "carving" of the candle or the insertion of the grains of incense, but not to forgo the text and some sign of honor to the candle. They have found that the text is best used after the lighting of the candle, perhaps just at the beginning of the procession.

In any case, the candle is lighted from the fire immediately after the prayer. Use adequate tools to do this. With a real bonfire, a feeble taper is going to melt. Acolytes take burning charcoal from the fire (again, find the right tool) and place them in the thuribles and add incense (some parishes have the presider throw a handful of incense into the fire itself during the prayer of blessing). The presider (or deacon) then is to take the candle and begin the processing, moving first to the door of the church. Acolytes with unlighted candles are alongside the minister carrying the candle; those with thuribles lead the procession.

At the door of the church (or at whatever point is convenient before the procession has moved too far from the fire), the minister lifts the candle high and sings: "Christ our light." And all respond: "Thanks be to God." If the one carrying the candle cannot chant these notes well, a cantor could stand beside the candle and sing.

Sometimes this first acclamation is preceded, in parishes where the carving of the candle was omitted, by the "Christ yesterday and today" text. This could be chanted but also can be shouted, proclaimed in loud and enthusiastic voices. The one holding the candle need not be the speaker. Those who later will be lectors (and this group naturally will be diverse: old and young, men and women) can divide up these lines and speak them in sequence from wherever each might be in the crowd around the fire or at the door of the church. During this, the lighted candle is held high. When using a number of speakers, the text can be expanded by repetition as appropriate. The "Amen" can be said first by one, then by several, then by all the speakers, and perhaps the whole assembly will join in on a last "Amen." Then immediately the minister or cantor sings the first "Light of Christ" (which seems to mean "Christ our light"). All involved must rehearse until this can be done—by heart, in the dark, letting each phrase ring out and yet all without a shade of theatrics. This is the kind of thing that will not be appropriate everywhere; when it is done so that it calls attention to the candle, not itself, then it should be retained every year, a steady part of the Vigil, a part that the assembly then can be at home with.

The procession enters the church (incense first, then candle, acolytes, the assembly, other ministers coming last). The rubrics suggest that the candles of all the people be lighted after the second "Light of Christ" and that all the church lights be turned on after the third "Light of Christ." It already has been suggested that the church lights not be turned on at all. If the candles of the assembly are to be lighted, then this can happen as people are entering the church, even beginning outside. There is nothing gained from dividing people up into those who light first, second and third. Or: Why light candles at all at this time? This may be the right question. The time for the lighting and holding of candles comes with the baptisms and the renewal of baptismal promises. Here the candles may be useful for finding one's place in the room, but that is all. They have to be extinguished during the whole liturgy of the word, then relighted. If the parish holds off on lighting the candles until the baptisms, candles can be distributed later (unless, as mentioned previously, parishioners bring their own new candles for the Vigil).

The sacramentary notes that another acclamation or another tone than the one given may be used in the procession. What is needed is an acclamation in this call-and-response format. Because the singing of all is vital to an acclamation, ministers should make every effort to encourage this. Before the second and third acclamations, the procession should stop and the minister with the candle turn to the assembly and raise the candle high, then wait for movement to cease and some silence. Sometimes the response

("Thanks be to God" or other) is best sung first by a cantor, then by everyone.

The sequence is repeated three times, then the candle is placed in its holder and the assembly finishes taking places in the room. During this time, the presider may bless the deacon, who is going to sing the Exsultet. Then the presider honors both the Easter candle and the book or scroll of the Exsultet with incense, clouds of incense. If there is no deacon who can sing the Exsultet worthily, then a singer is chosen who can chant this poem with beauty and great clarity in the words (this is a text no one will follow in a book or leaflet; the words must be clear).

For the Exsultet, the sacramentary may be placed on a lectern by the candle, but that would make one more piece of furniture. It is better if the singer can hold the book or if an acolyte can hold it (in which case the singer's arms are free for the usual gesture with the invitation to "Lift up your hearts"); other acolytes stand alongside holding candles for light. This should take place directly below the Easter candle. Some parishes have created a scroll or a special book where the Exsultet has been done in calligraphy; centuries ago, it was the practice in some local churches for these scrolls to include upside-down pictures of "this night" so that as the singing progressed, the pictures of the scroll were rolling down, right side up for the assembly to see in the candlelight.

The Exsultet is a once-a-year song, a treasure of the church. For most Catholics, it is their one encounter with the form of a eucharistic prayer outside the Mass. The Exsultet is placed here as climax to the rites of fire and candle that have taken us into these last hours of vigiling. This is a final gathering of forces for the night's vigil. There is an option for a "short form," but it is difficult to imagine the circumstances that would lead to this choice: There must be a good singer, else how could the church be keeping this Vigil in the first place? And with a good singer and a night when everyone there has chosen to come and keep vigil, why lose even a word of the text? The *Circular Letter* recognizes explicitly that— exactly as in the eucharistic prayer at Mass—it may be desirable to insert sung acclamations into the text of the Exsultet. Such acclamations must sound like what they are, one whole piece with the Exsultet itself.

The song is true to its name: It exults, even in English, with the nouns and verbs and adjectives that give this night definition: "Rejoice: heavenly powers, earth, church! This is our passover feast . . . This is the night . . . This is the night . . . This is the night . . . O happy fault, O necessary sin . . . The power of this holy night dispels all evil, washes guilt away, restores lost innocence, brings mourners joy; it casts out hatred, brings us peace, and humbles earthly pride. Night truly blessed when heaven is wedded to earth and we are reconciled with God." It is a victory song, a wedding song of God and humanity, earth and heaven. It is theology in its purest form, the song the church longs to sing. From the naming and acclamation of the night's deeds (as in "dispels all evil" and the list that follows) it is clear that the church understands this night to be sacramental. This text has many words and sentences that could well be heard again and be spoken about in the preaching of Eastertime.

After the assembly sings its Amen to the Exsultet, all are seated. Ministers sit so that they can give full attention to the lector. If the readings are to be done from the ambo, the acolytes can take tapers, light them from the Easter candle or other candles, and light whatever candles have been set up to provide light for the readers. They do this while people are settling into their places (and blowing out their candles if these were lighted during the beginning of the liturgy).

The Liturgy of the Word

This liturgy of the word is called by the sacramentary the "fundamental element of the Easter Vigil."

When all of the people are seated and all moving around has ceased, the presider may address the assembly with words that invite attention. The sacramentary's example of such a text is a model in its brevity, but not necessarily in its content. The direction might be more as follows:

> Dear friends, we are continuing our vigil and approaching its most solemn moments. Let us fasten on all these stories and songs, all these poems and exhortations. We have come hungry for God's word; here is our nourishment even as we gather strength to approach the font of baptism and the table of the eucharist.

One could say that the Vigil depends on the lectors. These readings are the foundation of the Vigil and the assembly depends on the readers to lay this foundation. It is hard to imagine that any lector could handle more than one reading tonight, so the parish's eight best lectors plus the gospel reader must be chosen well in advance with the understanding that they will attend rehearsals that will deal not only with each reading but also with the movements to and from the ambo (and possibly also with the candle acclamation described earlier).

Some parishes debate whether to include all of the readings. The *Circular Letter* includes this encouragement:

> Wherever possible, therefore, all the readings should be proclaimed, in order to preserve the character of the Easter Vigil, which of its nature should take a long time. (#85)

The *Letter* also suggests that an introduction to some or all of the readings may be given. There is no doubt that the right type of introduction can help people listen better, but that kind of introduction, delivered simply, is hard to find. It is too easy for many to slip into an approach to the readings from the Hebrew Scriptures that actually keeps the assembly from hearing what these readings really have to say. It is better to put every effort into the quality of the readings themselves, into the recitation or chanting of the prayers after each reading and into the homily.

The simplest question for those who would cut the number of readings would be: Where can you possibly cut?

Who would cut (or shorten) the reading of creation? This above all needs a fine reader. Our fasting of the first two days of Triduum should find us—is this hard to believe in our present world?—hungry to see the church's book opened tonight to its first page, and hungry then to hear the words at the head of all our scriptures: "In the beginning . . ."

Or the second reading, the hard story of Abraham and Isaac, who would cut this? Who would be willing to go without words and images like these: " 'Take your son Isaac whom you love' . . . with the wood he had cut for the holocaust . . . on the third day Abraham . . . 'God will provide the sheep for the holocaust' . . . as countless as the stars of the sky." As always, the lector's work is first to hear these words and dwell with them, then to help others so that they are amazed by a story like this.

The third reading is required, but no less powerful for that. It is the crossing of the sea and the drowning in the sea, and it is told in the old-fashioned way, with refrains scattered throughout: "Pharaoh and his chariots and charioteers" and "the water like a wall to their right and to their left." It is like anyone's story of great hardship and wonderment, but here the forging of a people. Some parishes suggest that Exodus 15:1 be omitted ("Then Moses and the Israelites sang this song to the Lord") in favor of Exodus 15:20–21 ("Then the prophet Miriam, Aaron's sister, took a tambourine in her hand; and all the women went out after her with tambourines and with dancing. And Miriam sang to them: Sing to the Lord . . ."). In any case, the reading can conclude in midsentence, with us ready to hear the song of Moses (or Miriam) and the singing takes up the canticle that follows. The canticle itself always is to be the song that follows this reading. (A Jewish commentary on these verses of scripture is a wonderful reflection, perhaps for the homilist: "When Miriam raised her voice in exultation, and the angels at the Throne of Glory began to take up the refrain, God rebuked them, saying: 'What! My children are drowning, and you would sing?' ")

The four readings from the prophetic books probably are the most often omitted. Yet without chapters 54 and 55 of Isaiah, we will not hear the images where love takes its complicated place in our night watch, love like that we may know best and hardest, love between a woman and a man. Here also is the call to come to the water and drink without paying, come to the table and feast, one and all alike. We are poor without such language. If we think that poetry like this is beyond the assembly and perhaps beyond the lector, enough time without such poetry will make our judgment come true. It takes poetry to know and love poetry. We can be certain, though, that receiving these passages, treasuring them in our hearts, is not a matter of education. Loving Isaiah and Baruch and Ezekiel's words doesn't come with a degree in literature. Words such as these live in the churches of the poor and "uneducated" now as they have and will, perhaps because there people are free to hunger for such words and more.

Ezekiel's images are more difficult (though the verses about the stony heart should be dear to us) and it is a temptation not so much to omit a reading as to substitute one of the stronger selections from the tradition (see page 109). Baruch offers no like temptation. Here at last is a strong feminine image of God, a name of God that is Wisdom: "All who hold her fast will live."

Today, there are parishes that add to these readings, especially following the tradition that would give us a long reading from the story of Noah, a substantial part of Jonah, the story from Daniel of the fiery furnace and the canticle that accompanies it, and the Song of Songs. Such an extended time is possible when the notion of Vigil—whether articulated or not—has taken root in the parish and people assemble tonight for a night watch and not for a little longer Mass. With this there can be an understanding that one need not remain the whole time: There is a freedom to move around, to go out awhile and return.

But embracing the whole lectionary—or more—tonight depends on believing that we do live by these words. It depends particularly on two very different aspects of such belief. First, we respect the Hebrew Scriptures: They clearly are tonight not obscure echoes of some gospel passage (as they often are treated in the Sunday lectionary), but they are our treasured texts, stories and poetry that have been handed on to us and that we will hand on, giving each generation the ground of its identity.

Second, to embrace this time of lengthy reading we have to believe that the spoken word, a reader with the book facing the assembly, remains a unique and powerful and, in fact, indispensable way for human beings to communicate. The church is made by what it hears. And what it hears is a human voice reading words from our book. They are old words, stories we have heard and poems we mostly remember. That is, of course, the point. Experience tells over and over that this can communicate as no technologically advanced media can. Experience also tells that this is not magic but work and devotion.

As in the usual Sunday pattern, there is some silence after each reading. The need for this is clear to anyone who experiences these texts well proclaimed. Then, also in the usual Sunday pattern, there is psalmody. If, as would be expected, several cantors and all the parish choirs are present tonight, then the singing will reflect all the various ways the parish is accustomed to singing the psalms. The parts of the assembly must be simple, some of them familiar from the psalms sung throughout the year. The *Circular Letter* is urgent that these be psalms and not other songs or loose paraphrases:

> After each reading a psalm is sung, to which the people respond. The melody for the responses should be such that it helps the participation and devotion of the faithful. The greatest care must be taken that trivial songs are not substituted in place of the psalms. (#86)

When a cantor leads the psalms, candles can be used in the same way as they are used for the lectors. When the choir needs light, careful planning is needed so that the light they need does not disrupt the quiet and dark. Accompaniment would normally be minimal.

As the psalm ends, the presider rises; the assembly also will stand (a rhythm in postures that flows through this part of the night). Immediately, the presider invites/demands: "Let us pray." Again, there is a silence, then two acolytes come to the presider, one with the book of prayers (sacramentary or book that has been prepared for the presider's use tonight), one with a candle. The prayer is spoken. The sacramentary texts for these prayers are not outstanding; others certainly will be given in the revision of the sacramentary. (See also the texts in the appendix, part 10.)

The last reading before the gospel is from the letter to the Romans. In the present sacramentary (to be revised, as noted, by the mid-1990s), the Gloria precedes this reading. This seems a relic of an understanding that the "Mass" now begins. In the experience of many parishes, the Gloria at this point breaks the rhythm of the readings, emphasizes the Gloria above the Alleluia and creates a needless division between the readings of the Hebrew Scriptures and those of the New Testament. There is another opinion about the Gloria, though. Martimort writes (in *The Church at Prayer,* Liturgical Press, volume four, page 43) that it is "the Christian Easter song . . . for a long time sung only during this holy night." There is no quarrel with that; only the placement seems a problem. Some have experimented with singing the Gloria later in the liturgy (e.g., during the sprinkling or after communion).

The reading from Romans is brief and direct. For the first time tonight, we hear the word "baptism." The words are "life," "death," "sin," "baptism," "crucified." Here, if anywhere, is a reading that requires a lector's long struggle with the text so that, in the end, the lector makes us hear, with something like amazed assent, Paul's fundamental profession of our faith.

The reading of the gospel is heralded with the return of the Alleluia. This happens in the once-a-year way of the Triduum. After the silence that follows the reading, the presider stands and the whole assembly stands. Then the Alleluia is sung three times by the cantor and each time repeated by the assembly. Each set is on a higher tone and the traditional melody—heard only this night—is used. The rubrics suggest that this be led by the presider, but only if it can be done well. The one chosen to sing the Exsultet might lead the Alleluia. There is no procession to the gospel during this—that comes in a moment. For now, it is as if the community can only stand alert and rejoice in the sound of this word not sung since before Ash Wednesday.

Augustine said this about the treasure that is this word come down to us from the Hebrew:

> O blessed Alleluia of heaven! No more anguish, no more adversity. No more enemy. No more love of destruction. Up above, praise to God, and here below, praise to God. Praise mingled with fear here, but without disturbance above. Here we chant in hope, there, in possession; here it is Alleluia *en route,* there it is Alleluia on arriving home.

The singing of Psalm 118 with the Alleluia refrain that will be used throughout Eastertime (and not beyond—though it might be the Alleluia used at funerals) then accompanies the procession of presider (or deacon) and acolytes with candles and incense. Normal Sunday practice could be followed, but it would not be out of place for this procession (and the singing of the psalm and Alleluia refrain) to take somewhat longer, perhaps circling through the assembly. A separate book of the gospels is not needed and, it can be argued, is a hindrance when we wish to show the importance of *all* the scripture in our book. The lectionary itself, however, brought to the presider by the lector after the chanted Alleluia, can be carried high by the presider. The significance here is not "getting a book from here to there." It is celebrating a book, dancing with this book, and especially on this night. The procession then honors not only the gospel but all the scriptures we have heard. After the long time of listening and silence, psalmody and prayer, the Alleluia and this procession come as high climax.

The announcement and reading of the gospel should be done with the same care and practice as the other readings. Sometimes the Alleluia refrain is repeated afterward as the acolytes return to their places. "After the gospel reading, the homily, even if short, is not to be omitted" (*Circular Letter,* #87). Homilists might prepare by reading, along with tonight's scriptures, the paschal homilies of John Chrysostom and others. Several of these homilies, including Chrysostom's, can be found in *A Triduum Sourcebook* (LTP), pages 111–14. Other exemplary texts are from the New Testament: The Romans reading we just now heard, or 1 Peter or 1 John. Gerard Sloyan argues that the homily is the time to draw together all the scriptures, rather than offering brief commentaries as the readings are done:

> Why do we recite a truncated history of Israel, indeed of the world since its creation, on this night of all nights? The culmination of this story in the Easter *kerygma* should make this clear. (*Pastoral Music,* August/ September 1989, page 18)

The homily is that *kerygma*.

The usual brief period of silence follows the homily. Then the pastor or the person most closely associated with the preparation of the elect comes forward to call the elect. In some places, this will be more powerful if the ambo and its microphone are not used. The elect only are called and they are called by name. They (with their godparents, who stand to one side) come around the person who has called them. Immediately, the cantor begins the litany of the saints. The procession of the elect, their godparents and the ministers now moves to the font. If the font is separated from the assembly and if there is room there for everyone, then all join the procession. The litany continues as long as necessary. Whatever tone is used, it should have the sense in its very sound of invoking the whole communion of the saints, all the holy ones of God, to walk with us now to these waters. The list of names of saints in the sacramentary should be increased with the patron saints of the parish and diocese and region and the patron saints of the elect. The latter parts of the litany should maintain the strength of the "pray for us" refrain, using "Lord, have mercy" or "Lord, hear our prayer" in settings familiar to the assembly.

The procession is vital: In a sense, the whole vigiling has taken place where the community could gather around this candle and book. Now the candle and the ministers (and the assembly when possible) are on the move, going solemnly, going with eagerness (at last we are at the waters) and, if we have listened to what Paul wrote, with some trepidation. The paschal candle leads the procession. The presider follows, then the elect and their godparents, then other ministers.

The Liturgy of Baptism

Every procession is about getting from here to there, but not primarily in space. "Here" and "there" are inside each person and the church itself. "Here" is the long vigiling in the dark of this night, reading scriptures. "There" is the font and the awesome deeds to take place there. It is still a long way. The litany can be sung rapidly but it should be long; it needs its time.

Whatever the place of the font, therefore, the procession should happen. If the font is near the ambo and altar, the procession forms and moves slowly through and around the chanting assembly. Even if the font is located at some distance, the procession need not take the shortest route. The timing of procession and litany should be well worked out in rehearsals.

The assembly stands to join in the litany. Each one—the elect excepted and probably the sponsors also because their hands are to be free—now lights her or his candle. The fire is spread from the paschal candle with the help of some of the acolytes. Wherever the font is, the assembly turns to face it.

At the font, some chaos is almost unavoidable if there are many to be baptized (in part because the elect are not to rehearse at all for this night). Ministers must stand clear of the sight lines of the assembly. The presider must be seen on the far side (from the assembly) of the font. The elect and godparents are nearby. One minister stands close to the presider and holds the sacramentary or prepared book of prayers. The litany continues (with some repetition if needed) until the presider is ready to bless the water.

The blessing of the water has, like the Exsultet, the nature of a eucharistic prayer: God is thanked and praised over this water. Some forms of the prayer provide for acclamations by the assembly. Like all acclamations, they are to be sung and are to be well integrated into the prayer. Such integration has two aspects. First, the placement of any acclamation must respect the structure of the prayer itself and not be random. Second, text and acclamation must flow; it should not seem like the presider chants a bit, then things stop and the assembly sings. This acclamation may be specific ("Springs of water, bless the Lord") or general ("All the earth proclaim the Lord"). It must be a text the assembly knows well, perhaps from

singing it every year on every Sunday of Easter as water is blessed and sprinkled.

The full gestures—breathing on the water, plunging the paschal candle into the water, splashing the water at times so that its sound is heard by those who cannot see it—are needed. This is to be a powerful text powerfully proclaimed in word and gesture.

What happens next depends on whether adults are being baptized, on their number and on the manner of baptism. In what is becoming the normal practice, the first adult to be baptized now enters the baptismal pool. In many parishes, the presider also enters. The task at hand is the final and decisive questioning of the elect. First are the renunciations, then the affirmation of faith. When there are only a few (perhaps ten or fewer) to be baptized, the presider can question them one at a time after each has entered the font (or when baptism is still by pouring water at a small font, when each has come forward to stand before the presider). The presider asks by name: "Helen, do you renounce . . ."

When there are a dozen or more to be baptized, the renunciation questions can be asked once, but then each person, one at a time, replies (there always is some loss when the questions cannot be asked of each person by name.) The first of the elect enters the font only when the renunciations are completed. Then each is questioned by name, affirms the faith and is baptized. Only when the number is truly large (perhaps more than 20) would the affirmations not be repeated by each person.

Under no circumstances should these renunciations and affirmations be omitted or shortened. If anything, the texts are too brief for the work they have to do. In periods where the catechumenate flourished, and in the Orthodox churches today, the crucial moments here are marked by gestures and words that leave no doubt. Our own rite should be as strong as possible: Here, after months and years of preparation, is the decision. Here whole ways of living and deciding and understanding are left behind—and not just left behind: thrown out, ejected, rejected, sent packing. This is to be heard in the way the questions are asked. It then will be heard in how they are answered. Alexander Schmemann has written of the renunciations:

> The first act of the Christian life is a renunciation, a challenge. No one can be Christ's until he has, first, faced evil, and then, become ready to *fight* it. How far is this spirit from the way in which we often proclaim, or to use a more modern term, "sell" Christianity today. Is it not usually presented as a comfort, help, release from tensions, a reasonable investment of time, energy and money? . . . How could we then speak of *fight* when the very setup of our churches must, by definition, convey the idea of softness, comfort, peace? (*Of Water and the Spirit,* St. Vladimir's Seminary Press, page 86)

The longer form of the renunciations usually offers a better image of what is happening here. The presider asks the questions directly to the elect, looking at each person and not at the book, speaking in a loud voice because the whole church must hear and witness. Presiders should commit the questions to memory—indeed, these are questions all the baptized should know by heart.

When baptism is by immersion or submersion, a decision must be made about the garments of the elect. In some parishes, they come tonight wearing old clothes, knowing these will be changed later. Other parishes ask the elect to wear bathing clothes, then give them plain, ample robes to wear during the first part of the service (in color and texture, these robes are not to resemble the baptismal garments). These robes then are removed and the elect go into the font wearing bathing garments. Still other parishes give the elect such plain robes to wear over their underwear throughout the first part of the service. They then are baptized in these garments.

The approach should be based on common sense: What will not distract either the elect or the assembly from what is being done here? What will be the fullest possible sign of one way left behind and another embraced, the fullest possible sign that there is a death that happens here in these waters, a washing and a drowning, and on the other side, life in Christ? For wonderful commentary on the renunciations and the stripping of garments, see Cyril of Jerusalem's words to the newly baptized *(A Triduum Sourcebook,* LTP, pages 121–22).

After so much and so long, the text and deed to baptize are so simple. Three times a full bucket or pitcher (or some other useful and simple vessel of water) is scooped from the font and poured over the head of each of the elect as the words are proclaimed, "N., I baptize you in the name of the Father, and of the Son and of the Holy Spirit." That's all. That is truly all.

Immediately, while the newly baptized still stands in the water, the assembly acclaims what has happened (e.g., "You have put on Christ, in Christ you have been baptized, alleluia, alleluia"). The tune and words should be known well, should sound like an acclamation, should be sung by people who look in each face of these newly baptized. In doing so, each Christian truly affirms her or his own baptism, knows as at no other moment that we all have crossed over. Here in this watery tomb we died. Here is the church born, from this watery womb. Here is our wedding, loved and graced by God. Death, life, wedding and more: The font and its waters, the words of baptism, the acclamation must make it clear.

> So radically incomparable is this transformation in Christ-become-life-giving-Spirit that only the most primal human experiences such as marriage, birth, death, and dining together offer clues to it. (Aidan Kanavagh, *The Shape of Baptism*, Pueblo/Liturgical Press, page 30)

That immersion or submersion are the preferred forms of baptism is clear from the RCIA (e.g., #226). But it is not a matter of authority so much as simple clarity about what is going on. Drawing on the scripture, Aidan Kavanagh writes further:

> While one obviously could wash without bathing as one could eat without dining, both acts took on vastly enriched social and personal importance as they were ritualized, becoming freighted with more than merely utilitarian meaning in the process. The surviving Roman baths found through the Mediterranean area, Europe, and the Middle East testify to this. The New Testament corpus brings both this social pattern and the religious washing and bathing patterns found in Judaism to bear as it seeks to express what adherence to Christ in the Spirit means for Christian faith and practice. Receiving the Spirit through Christ is likened to a *birth bath* in John 3:3–5 and Titus 3:5–7; to a *funeral bath* and burial in Romans 6:1–11; to a bride's *nuptial bath* in Ephesians 5:26. These cultural practices were consummated in anointing and in arraying

the body in clean, new, or otherwise special clothing (Galatians 3:27) as the final stages of the bath itself. *(The Shape of Baptism,* Pueblo/ Liturgical Press, pages 28–29)

The images are birth, funeral, wedding. They come again and again, but without real water, real bathing, they are missed.

In those places where there is no immersion font, those to be baptized come forward to the small font one at a time; after answering the questions, they bend deeply over the font and the presider pours water in abundance (water splashing to the floor is called for by the fullness needed). The baptized should be positioned so that when they again stand straight, they are facing the assembly. While the acclamation is sung, the newly baptized should simply remain standing in the sight of the assembly. All ministers and godparents should be out of the sight lines of the assembly.

Each newly baptized Christian is helped from the waters by sponsor and others, is wrapped with a towel and taken to the side. Children of catechetical age are to be baptized (and confirmed) with the adults. Infants may be baptized at the vigil, but many parishes baptize infants on Easter morning. When all the baptisms are completed, the elect are given their baptismal garments ("N. and N., you have become a new creation . . ."). Also at this time, a candle is lighted from the Easter candle for each of the newly baptized; this is done by the godparent who presents the candle as the presider says, "You have been enlightened . . ." Usually, the newly baptized then leave to take off their wet clothes and put on their baptismal garments.

While they are drying themselves or changing clothes, the presider can address the whole assembly (including any to be received into full communion) with the renewal of renunciations and affirmations. Then, while the assembly sings a baptismal song, which may be a repeat of the acclamation after each baptism, the presider and other ministers scoop buckets of water from the font, take evergreen branches and proceed to sprinkle the assembly thoroughly. In some parishes, as an alternative, all come forward singing (much as on Good Friday to the cross), to place their hands in this water and sign themselves with the cross.

This renewal of baptismal promises is not central to the liturgy and it is not ancient. Where the assembly has just baptized, this should flow from the true affirmation that has just been witnessed and acclaimed. But the renewal will come to be in the witnessing and the acclamation; it will not need questions and answers.

Then those to be received into full communion are called by name. They come forward, carrying the lighted candles they have held since the litany. In the simple form presented in the RCIA (#585), they affirm their faith in the life and teaching of the Roman Catholic Church.

The National Statutes for the Catechumenate (U.S. bishops, 1986) say clearly:

> It is preferable that reception into full communion not take place at the Easter Vigil lest there be any confusion of such baptized Christians with the candidates for baptism, possible misunderstanding of or even reflection upon the sacrament of baptism celebrated in another Church or ecclesial community, or any perceived triumphalism in the liturgical welcome into the Catholic eucharistic community.

This is a well-taken caution. It is difficult, however, to reconcile what it suggests with any desire that the celebration of confirmation accompany reception into full communion. The United States edition of the RCIA contains a "Celebration at the Easter Vigil of the Sacraments of Initiation and of the Rite of Reception into the Full Communion of the Catholic Church." Obviously, there is some presumption that reception will take place at the Vigil. (Note that this order of service, beginning at #566 in the RCIA, provides the norm for this part of the Vigil when there are both baptisms and receptions into full communion.)

The newly received remain in front of the assembly until the newly baptized join them. Their sponsors now can hold their candles during the confirmation.

The confirmation ritual is brief. It is a sealing of this baptism with the laying on of hands and the anointing with fragrant chrism. Usually, both the newly baptized and those who have just been received into full communion now are confirmed. They all face the assembly. The presider invites prayer (the assembly still stands with lighted candles), then extends hands over those to be confirmed and prays aloud. Next the presider goes to each one, laying hands on them (the godparent—or sponsor for those received into full communion—may stand behind with a hand on the shoulder of the one being confirmed). This laying on of hands should not be rushed. It is done in silence, perhaps with the assembly softly singing an ostinato. Then the presider lifts up the bowl of chrism and goes to each person, anointing each one with a generous amount of chrism. The chrism should be poured or smeared on the top of the head, not just the forehead. The chrism is not wiped off but later should be rubbed into the hair and skin by the newly confirmed. When all have been anointed, the assembly can repeat the baptismal acclamation. This, rather than applause, will give a true sense of acclaiming what has happened and not simply the persons to whom it has happened. (Also, applause is impossible if, as is best, the assembly still holds lighted candles.) The singing of this acclamation can accompany all the newly confirmed as they return to places in the assembly.

When baptism is by immersion and when there is no one to be received into full communion at this liturgy, confirmation might best follow immediately after baptism and before changing clothes and putting on the baptismal garments. This allows for a much fuller use of the chrism because it can be poured over the head without any risk of staining good clothes. The newly baptized and confirmed then leave to change clothes while the assembly renews the renunciations and affirmations and is sprinkled with water.

These rites have a gravity that must not be destroyed by a casual or joking tone. Working with water and oil like this, things can happen that cause laughter. That is expected and in place. There will also be tears. These are also expected and in place. After all, this is birth and this is death and we are not in control. What is not in place is the presider who treats everything lightly. There is bound to be spontaneity in these rites, but it will destroy them unless it takes place within the flow of an order of service that each minister involved knows thoroughly.

The prayers of intercession, sung if possible, conclude the whole liturgies of word and baptism. For the newly baptized, it is the first time to join the church in its work of interceding. Until now, they have been dismissed before this moment. Perhaps it is difficult for us to understand the meaning of this as we have attached little importance to the work of intercession. Still there is insight for us in the discipline of those periods when the unbaptized never joined in intercession and the baptized saw intercession as both the privilege and the duty that went with baptism. The baptized were to be the voice reminding God of the poor and the church and the troubles of the world. It was practically a job description. So this first time to join in our intercession is not a minor moment in the initiation; its strength will depend entirely on how well the church intercedes Sunday by Sunday and day by day.

Then all extinguish their candles and are seated while the table is prepared for the celebration of the eucharist.

Liturgy of the Eucharist

This is the eucharist of the Triduum. Long before eucharist was celebrated as part of the Holy Thursday observance, before there was any communion rite as part of Good Friday, this was *the* eucharist of Triduum. Perhaps it will be so again. The fasting for two days now brings us to this table.

If there is good Sunday practice for the preparation of the table, for the eucharistic prayer and for the communion rite, then little must be different tonight. If tonight is different because the bread has been baked in the parish or because everyone can share the cup, then something is right tonight but wrong on Sundays.

The RCIA suggests that the bread and wine be carried forward from the assembly by the newly baptized. Also, it calls attention to the inserts in Eucharistic Prayers I, II and III. These inserts are found in the sacramentary under "Ritual Masses: Baptism." If used, the text should be copied and inserted in place so that the turning of pages can be avoided during the eucharistic prayer.

The final suggestion in the RCIA (#293 and #594) is that: "Before saying 'This is the Lamb of God,' the celebrant briefly may remind the neophytes of the preeminence of the eucharist, which is the climax of their initiation and the center of the whole Christian life."

This is an often-missed rubric. The importance is not that the presider actually insert some comment. That, in fact, probably should be nothing more than an additional phrase in the usual invitation:

> This is the Lamb of God, who takes away the sins of the world. Come, all you who have passed through the waters and have been clothed in Christ. Come with joy, come at last to the banquet table of the Lord. Happy are those who are called to this supper.

What is not so easy is establishing a sense in the newly baptized and in the whole church that eucharist is the climax of initiation. Even the placement of this rubric about reminding the neophytes of the preeminence of the eucharist, relating it to the communion rite rather than the eucharistic prayer, indicates how deep is the problem. Eucharist is not communion, is not the bread and the cup. Eucharist is the whole action of the assembly that begins with the invitation to "Lift up your hearts." But our failure here is logical: We do not yet celebrate this way Sunday by Sunday. The eucharistic prayer is not known as the central deed of the assembly. We still act as observers during the eucharistic prayer. Our failure is witnessed by the ease with which, on Sundays, we bring hosts from the tabernacle for the communion of the assembly. If we understood the eucharistic deed of the baptized, we could not do this.

So while the RCIA's reminder not to forget eucharist as part of initiation is well taken, the answer is not so easy as that suggested. Perhaps the Vigil each year now can serve in this way: to make us confront our failure with the primary symbol, the eucharist that is the deed of thanksgiving to God, the deed of sacrifice and of offering, the deed of sanctification, the deed of the assembly of baptized people. Perhaps each year's Vigil will find a parish closer to that solid, Sunday-by-Sunday practice where it is clear without saying an extra word that eucharist is the climax of initiation, tonight and every Lord's Day.

Tonight's eucharistic liturgy, then, follows this general form. Good bread and wine are brought forth; as usual, there is time to collect money for the church and the poor. The cloth might be spread at this time, and the table is prepared. This is done with reverence and simplicity; it is a time to catch one's breath.

Then the presider goes to the table and invites all: "Lift up your hearts." The dialogue and the acclamations make a strong and integral part of the prayer. At one period, it was forbidden to kneel (or fast) during Eastertime. So the assembly might take that active and attentive posture of standing during the eucharistic prayer, but only if this can be done without lengthy explanations and instructions; again, it is the Sunday-by-Sunday practice that needs work here.

When the Amen has concluded the eucharistic prayer, the Lord's Prayer is chanted or recited as usual. Its words need no comment; for the newly baptized and their godparents and perhaps for others, they will come as the great summary of the church's prayer, the simple gift of the baptized to the elect, truly known by heart. The kiss of peace, like the intercessions, is another "first" for the newly baptized. In the centuries when the catechumenate flourished, much was made of this first kiss. Its place in the liturgy has varied, and some today would place it at the conclusion of the anointing with chrism or after the intercessions. This is done to emphasize that now, at last, this peace is given to these people who have been so long dismissed. Departures from the normal Sunday practice should be done only reluctantly, however. The danger, whether the peace is given now or earlier, is that it becomes a "congratulations" or a "happy Easter."

All attention returns to the table for that which gave our gathering its first name, the breaking of the bread. One could hope that the newly baptized, seeing this as if for the first time, would somehow come up with this name all over again. When communion ministers have brought cups and plates to the table, filled them and gone to their communion stations, the presider holds out bread and cup and makes the invitation. The communion procession and song begin at once. The song probably should be the same here each year; it might well have many alleluias as a refrain.

The neophytes come to communion first, but there should not be any sense of division (as there is when ministers of communion or concelebrating clergy receive communion before the assembly). The move should be directly from the invitation ("This is the Lamb of God") to the procession and song.

After the procession, there should be a short time of silence and stillness, then the quiet prayer after communion. The blessing follows (#6 of the Solemn Blessings is for the Vigil and Easter Sunday, but it is not an especially strong text). Then comes the dismissal with alleluias, then the procession (of the newly baptized and their godparents and families, along with the ministers and, if possible, the whole assembly) to the place of breaking the fast and further rejoicing. Milk and honey, once served to the newly baptized with their first communion, could be the basis for the food and drink at this breakfast.

Easter Sunday

The Triduum ends with the Evening Prayer of Sunday. The days of Eastertime also begin with this Sunday, the first of the 50 days that will climax at Pentecost. The season springs from the Triduum, as the *General Norms for the Liturgical Year and the Calendar* say: "The 50 days from Easter Sunday to Pentecost are celebrated in joyful exultation as one feast day, or better as one 'great Sunday' (Athanasius)." It is as if the third and last day of the Triduum cannot be brought to an end: On it goes as a wonderful mystagogia, an unfolding of the mysteries celebrated at the Vigil.

For this to be so in parish life, more and more members of the church will have to love the Triduum and celebrate the great Vigil together. For good reason the *General Norms,* when outlining the liturgical year, begin with the Triduum, go on to talk about Eastertime, and only then discuss Lent. That is the way it works. The things we do in Triduum need the 50 days to play themselves out; the things we do in Triduum need the 40 days of preparation.

But we are a people of commitments and conveniences and of many calendars. The notion of a night in church—no options, this night or none at all—is nearly beyond us. A difficult part of restoring the Triduum in our culture is this: We believe that time is ours to do with as we wish or as the demands of economic and social life dictate to us. We do not believe that time is God's, that God's good time makes its own demands, that a certain Thursday night comes and we simply stop everything else and observe the discipline of the Triduum.

As it is, Easter may be seen as an important feast, even an important day to celebrate as a community, but little more. We find it hard to make the kind of transformation in outlook that the Triduum not only invites but demands. When that transformation does happen, it is rarely because someone read a book or attended a seminar. Rather, it happens when the parish community, year after year, has begun to act this way. We grope our way here. None of us knows much. We make these life-and-death rites our own, these rehearsals for living the lives of baptized people. We trust the church, in a way, to hand on to us the mysteries.

We might hope that some day a whole parish will attend their Vigil. When the great breakfast ends and the sun is up (and perhaps Morning Prayer has been sung), it is time to rest and then to gather again in the late afternoon around the font to celebrate the paschal Vespers. Morning Masses are not then necessary. What will be necessary in large parishes is a place where everyone can gather for such a Vigil; that will be a pleasant problem to have.

For now, we might look on the Easter Sunday morning Masses as the first Masses of the Easter season. They are not to be abbreviated versions of the Vigil for those who didn't make it. The room (not just the area in front) is filled with the Easter flowers. The paschal candle burns continuously (until the completion of Evening Prayer on Sunday) and the font somehow invites all to approach and take some of the water. The entrance rites should be what they will be throughout the Easter season (except today the baptismal promises are added), for example:

Morning Masses

Sign of the cross and greeting

Invitation and renewal of baptismal renunciations and affirmations

Thanksgiving over the Easter water (e.g., Prayer C in the sacramentary)

Song during a thorough sprinkling of the assembly

Gloria (unless this is sung during the sprinkling)

Opening prayer

In some parishes, the ministers begin at the font or other place where the water is. There is no procession and no "entrance song" because procession and song come within the rite. Several ministers, especially persons involved in the initiation work that climaxed at the Vigil, can assist the presider, each taking a branch and going with an acolyte (who holds a bucket of water just taken from the font) to one aisle or one area of the room. This order differs from the sacramentary where the renewal of baptismal promises and the sprinkling comes after the homily. That has its advantages; the above order simply does on Easter Sunday what will be done on all the other Sundays of the season.

In preparing the liturgies of Easter Sunday, many parishes will need to attend closely to the following:

- Hospitality. If numbers of visitors are expected: greeters and ushers must be prepared; perhaps a special handout is placed in the bulletin saying words of welcome and telling about the parish; sometimes the communion invitation needs a few words of clarification about communion under both forms.

- Music. This is not the time for introducing new music but for the music everyone can sing, probably the music they sang all through last Eastertime, and some hymns that will be familiar to all the visitors.

- Excellence in all the ministries. One hopes for this every Sunday but should make certain of it today.

- Hospitality afterward for parishioners and visitors alike.

As mentioned previously, Easter Sunday might be one of the days appointed for infant baptisms at one or all of the morning liturgies. In keeping with the lenten season, no baptisms have been celebrated for 40-plus days. If infant baptisms are to take place, parents with infants and their godparents could assemble to be near the presider and to be introduced and questioned in the entrance rite. The baptisms themselves take place as usual, after the homily. Then, even where the sprinkling will take place in the entrance rite during the rest of Eastertime, today the renewal of baptismal renunciations and affirmations along with the sprinkling of the assembly takes place following the baptisms.

The newly baptized are to be remembered in the intercessions today and on all Sundays of the Easter season. When they are present on these Sundays, they are to have special places (according to the RCIA, #248).

The whole of Eastertime should see the parish's best effort to bake altar bread and provide a good wine for communion. First communions are in place today and on all the Sundays of Easter.

These morning liturgies are a time to bless the Easter foods and baskets of Easter eggs. If parishioners are encouraged to bring large baskets of festive Easter foods, they will need tables and the ushers' help in arranging these baskets during the Mass. There is an "Order of the Blessing of Food for the First Meal of Easter" in the *Book of Blessings* (#1701-23), but the only text needed for the blessing during Mass would be #1716. This can follow the prayer after communion and precede the final blessing. The full rite of blessing Easter food could be used today apart from the Mass.

The conclusion of Easter Mass adds the double Alleluia to the dismissal. This is intended for singing; if spoken, it needs some energy to bring a good response.

Paschal Vespers

From the first, the reestablishment of the Triduum has been linked to the celebration of Paschal Vespers, that is, Evening Prayer of the community on Sunday. But even those parishes that have made great efforts with the keeping of the Triduum have been reluctant to begin this liturgy. Some have done so and have found it beautiful but little attended. A few places have had greater success, making beginnings at a habit: The newly baptized and their godparents and families know that this is part of the initiation, and others who have experienced the power of the initiation rites begin to come. (One parish has an annual Easter egg hunt late Sunday afternoon for the children, then parents and children join others for Vespers.) Numbers are not the issue, except that we want more people to find how peaceful and joyous this ending of the Triduum can be. It is best to decide to do Paschal Vespers well, expect just a few people, and not worry.

Some would argue that this one more liturgy is one too many, especially for those who have taken responsibility all along. Often, however, the experience is quite the opposite: Especially for those who have borne the responsibility for the liturgy of the Triduum, Vespers can come as great delight. This time can be so filled with contemplation, with joy and with a certain sense of farewell to the Triduum. The last is not unlike the melancholy of observant Jews in the rites of a Saturday evening when the Sabbath takes its leave of the household. But here our farewell is filled with joy in the 50 days that prolong our rejoicing in the paschal mystery we have entered.

Following is a rather full form for Paschal Vespers. It may be seen more as a goal than a beginning point. It readily admits of simplification as long as its principal elements are kept: the presence of the paschal candle and the thanksgiving for the light, at least some psalmody and some Alleluia antiphons, the procession to the font and taking water from the font, an appropriate reading, the Lord's Prayer, some hymnody. Such a simplified Paschal Vespers is found in *A Triduum Sourcebook* (LTP), pages 158–63.

The following introduction and outline is taken from the 1992 edition of *Sourcebook for Sundays and Seasons* (LTP) by Thomas Ryan.

The liturgical books and their commentaries (the *Circular Letter,* #98; the *Ceremonial of Bishops,* #371; and the *Liturgy of the Hours,* #213) advocate the restoration of "Baptismal Vespers" to complete the Triduum. It requires a well-celebrated and well-attended Triduum before it, but a vibrant celebration of the Triduum without it seems incomplete.

Ansgar Chupungco in *Liturgies of the Future* devotes much attention to this celebration and its history (pages 175–84). It is a stational liturgy, meaning that all move from one location or "station" in the church complex to another. In medieval Rome, the Christians, at their cathedral, went in procession from one building to the next, from the eucharistic space to the baptismal space to the chrismation space. "The stational Vespers of Easter Sunday thus can

be regarded as a ritual recalling . . . of the paschal sacraments of baptism, confirmation and eucharist."

This outline is suggested:

- The paschal candle has been kept burning all day. All gather nearby, with booklet and taper.

- Service of light (found, for example, in GIA's *Worship*) begins. All candles of the assembly and of the church are lit from the paschal candle. No electric lights are turned on, to emphasize the gathering shadows of evening.

- Opening dialogue.

- Hymn praising Easter light, sung by all. The traditional hymn, "At the Lamb's high feast," is found with two tunes in *Worship*.

- Thanksgiving for light, sung by the cantor. Easter texts are available in GIA's *Praise God in Song*.

- The assembly's candles can be extinguished and any necessary light turned on for the psalmody. The appointed psalms for Easter Sunday have wonderful antiphons. [Note: Psalm 114, "When Israel went out of Egypt" is appropriate and holds a special place in the psalmody of Eastertime.]

- During the New Testament canticle from Revelation, a congregational Alleluia should be repeated often; cantors sing the verses. This is the music to accompany a procession of all to the font. The shortest route does not have to be taken. All follow the incense bearer, a minister bearing the paschal candle and the presider. [Note: Be sure that it is possible to carry the paschal candle, which has been burning all day; the pool of melted wax may make this difficult.]

- Depending on the size and location of the baptistry, all remain there until after the baptismal commemoration or until the end of the service.

- Hebrews 10:12–14, or the gospel about the Emmaus experience (Lectionary, #47, at the end of the Easter pericopes), or John 20:19–23 (the appearance of Jesus on the evening of the first day of the week) or a patristic selection from the Easter octave may be read.

- A homily revels in the Easter symbols around us.
- Silence.
- Responsorial song or the proper responsory listed at Easter Sunday Evening Prayer.
- Prayer over the blessed Easter water (adapted from RCIA, #222D or #222E; or from option C of the sacramentary's sprinkling rite).
- All approach the font and sign themselves and each other. Those unable to reach high enough or stoop low enough can be helped by those nearby. Meanwhile, all sing an antiphon such as the one from the blessing of water at the Vigil.
- The Magnificat is sung with its proper antiphon as all are honored with incense.
- Intercessions can be drawn from the *Liturgy of the Hours*.
- Lord's Prayer.
- Prayer of Easter.
- Solemn blessing of the day.
- Dismissal with the traditional sung double Alleluia.
- Recessional hymn sung by all. "Come, ye faithful, raise the strain" would provide a rousing conclusion.

Chapter 50 of the *Book of Blessings* is entitled: "Order for the Blessing of Homes during the Christmas and Easter Seasons." This provides a rite that is especially helpful in those communities where it has long been customary for homes to be blessed on Easter or during the Easter season. The *Circular Letter* suggests that part 2 of chapter 1 in the *Book of Blessings* is also appropriate. This is the "Order for the Annual Blessing of Families in Their Own Homes." It includes this rubric:

Blessing of Homes

> Pastors and their assistants must therefore consider as a sacred trust the custom of an annual visit, particularly during the Easter season, to the

families living in their parish. The occasion is a rich opportunity to fulfill pastoral responsibilities that grow in effectiveness the more the priests come to know the families. (#69)

The bishops of the United States in the 1980s prepared and published a ritual for all members of the church, *Catholic Household Blessings and Prayers*. This contains daily prayers, including table prayers for the Triduum (page 82) and Easter season (pages 84–89), as well as other ways that these days can be observed by individuals and households (pages 143–51). There is a Blessing of Easter Foods (page 152) and a Blessing of Homes during Eastertime (page 153). This book can be given as a parish gift to all those newly baptized and newly received, to the parents of infants who are being baptized, to the newly married, to the families of children receiving first communion. In every case there should be some catechesis about how this book can be used in the home (the book's introduction will be helpful). Especially in the Easter season, such catechesis—even in the homilies—is a part of showing how the mysteries we have celebrated in the Triduum are to be the pattern of our daily lives, brought there by the good habits of Catholic ritual and prayer.

Appendix: Part One
A Rite of Passage

Aidan Kavanagh is professor of liturgy at the Divinity School of Yale University. He told the following story within a lecture delivered in August 1977 at the Theology Institute held at Holy Cross Abbey in Colorado. It is reprinted, with the author's kind permission, to give us hope for the Vigil in this time of liturgical renewal.

I have always rather liked the gruff robustness of the first rubric for baptism found in a late fourth-century church order that directs that the bishop enter the vestibule of the baptistry and say to the catechumens without commentary or apology only four words: "Take off your clothes." There is no evidence that the assistants fainted or the catechumens asked what he meant. Catechesis and much prayer and fasting had led them to understand that the language of their passage this night in Christ from death to life would be the language of the bathhouse and the tomb—not that of the forum and the drawing room.

So they stripped and stood there, probably faint from fasting, shivering from the cold of early Easter morning and with awe at what was about to transpire. Years of formation were about to be consummated; years of having their motives and lives scrutinized; years of hearing the word of God read and expounded at worship; years of being dismissed with prayer before the faithful went on to celebrate the eucharist; years of having the doors to the assembly hall closed to them; years of seeing the tomb-like baptistry building only from without; years of hearing the old folks of the community tell hair-raising tales of what being a Christian had cost their own grandparents when the emperors were still pagan; years of running into a reticent and reverent vagueness concerning what actually was done by the faithful at the breaking of bread and in that closed baptistry. Tonight all this was about to end as they stood there naked on a cold floor in the gloom of this eerie room.

Abruptly the bishop demands that they face westward, toward where the sun dies swallowed up in darkness, and denounce the King of shadows and death and things that go bump in the night. Each one of them comes forward to do this loudly under the hooded gaze of the bishop (who is tired from presiding all night at the Vigil continuing next door in the church), as deacons shield the nudity of the male catechumens from the women, and as deaconesses screen the women in the same manner. This is when each of them finally lets go of the world and of life as they have known it: The umbilical cord is cut, but they have not yet begun to breathe.

Then they must each turn eastward toward where the sun surges up bathed in a light that just now can be seen stealing into the alabaster windows of the room. They must voice their acceptance of the King of light and life who has trampled down death by his own death. As each one finishes this, he or she is fallen upon by a deacon or a deaconess who vigorously rubs olive oil into the catechumen's body, as the bishop perhaps dozes off briefly, leaning on his cane. (He is like an old surgeon waiting for the operation to begin.)

When all the catechumens have been thoroughly oiled, they and the bishop are suddenly startled by the crash of the baptistry doors being thrown open. Brilliant golden light spills out into the shadowy vestibule, and following the bishop (who has now regained his composure), the catechumens and the assistant presbyters, deacons, deaconesses and sponsors move into the most glorious room that most of them have ever seen. It is a high, arbor-like pavilion of green, gold, purple and white mosaic from marble floor to domed ceiling, sparkling like jewels in the light of innumerable oil lamps that fill the room with heady warmth. The windows are beginning to blaze with the light of Easter dawn. The walls curl with vines and tendrils that thrust up from the floor, and at their tops, apostles gaze down robed in snow-white togas, holding crowns. These apostles stand around a golden chair draped with purple on which rests only an open book. And above all these, in the highest point of the ballooning dome, a naked Jesus (very much in the flesh) stands up to his waist in the Jordan as an unkempt John pours water on him, and God's disembodied hand points the Holy Spirit at Jesus' head in the form of a white bird.

Suddenly the catechumens realize that they have unconsciously formed themselves into a mirror image of this lofty icon on the floor directly beneath it. They are standing around a pool in the middle of the floor, into which gushes water pouring noisily from the mouth of a stone lion crouching atop a pillar at poolside. The bishop stands beside this, his presbyters on each side: A deacon has entered the pool, and the other assistants are trying to maintain a modicum of decorum among the catechumens who forget their nakedness as they crowd close to see. The room is warm and humid, and it glows. It is a golden paradise in a bathhouse in a mausoleum: an oasis, Eden restored: the navel of the world, where death and life meet, copulate and become undistinguishable from each other. Jonah peers out from a niche, Noah from another, Moses from a third, the paralytic carrying his stretcher from a fourth. The windows begin to sweat.

The bishop rumbles a massive prayer—something about the Spirit and the waters of life and death—and then pokes the water a few times with his cane. The catechumens recall Moses doing something like that to a rock from which water flowed, and they are mightily impressed. Then a young male catechumen of about ten, the son of pious parents, is led down into the pool by the deacon. The water is warm (it has been heated in a furnace), and the oil on his body spreads out on the surface in iridescent swirls. The deacon positions the child near the cascade from the lion's mouth. The bishop leans over on his cane and, in a voice that sounds like something out of the Apocalypse, says: "Euphemius! Do you believe in God the Father, who created all of heaven and earth?" After a nudge from the deacon beside him, the boy murmurs that he does. And just in time, for the deacon, who has been doing this for 50 years and is the boy's grandfather, wraps him in his arms, lifts him backward into the rushing waters and forces him under the surface. The old deacon smiles through his beard at the wide brown eyes that look up at him in shock and fear from beneath the water (the boy has purposely not been told what to expect). Then he raises him up coughing and sputtering. The bishop waits until the boy can speak again, and leaning over a second time, tapping the boy on the shoulder with his cane, says: "Euphemius! Do you believe in Jesus Christ, God's only Son, who was conceived of the Virgin Mary, suffered under Pontius Pilate, and was crucified, died and was buried? Who rose on the third day and ascended into heaven, from whence he will come again to judge the living and the dead?" This time the boy replies like a shot, "I do," and then holds his nose. "Euphemius! Do you believe in the Holy Spirit, the master and giver of life, who proceeds from the Father, who is to be honored and glorified equally with the Father and the Son, who spoke by the prophets? And in one holy, catholic and apostolic church which is the communion of God's holy ones? And in the life that is coming?" "I do."

When the boy comes up the third time, his vast grandfather gathers him in his arms and carries him up the steps leading out of the pool. There another deacon roughly dries Euphemius with a warm towel, and a senior presbyter, who is almost 90 and is regarded by all as a "confessor" because he was imprisoned for the faith as a young man, tremulously pours perfumed oil from a glass pitcher over the boy's damp head until it soaks his hair and runs down over his upper body. The fragrance of this enormously expensive oil fills the room as the old man mutters: "God's servant, Euphemius, is anointed in the name of the Father, Son and Holy Spirit." Euphemius then is wrapped in a new linen tunic; the fragrant chrism seeps into it, and he is given a burning terra-cotta oil lamp and told to go stand by the door and keep quiet. Meanwhile, the other baptisms have continued.

When all have been done in this same manner (an old deaconess, a widow, replaced Euphemius's grandfather when it came the women's time), the clergy strike up the Easter hymn, "Christ is risen from the dead, he has crushed death by his death and bestowed life on those who lay in the tomb." To this constantly repeated melody interspersed with the psalm verse, "Let God arise and smite his enemies," the whole baptismal party—tired, damp, thrilled and oily—walk out into the blaze of Easter morning and go next door to the church led by the bishop. There he bangs on the closed doors with his cane: They are flung open, the endless vigil is halted and the baptismal party enters as all take up the hymn "Christ is risen . . .", which is all but drowned out by the ovations that greet Christ truly risen in his newly born ones. As they enter, the fragrance of chrism fills the church: It is the Easter smell, God's grace olfactorally incarnate. The pious struggle to get near the newly baptized to touch their chrismed hair and rub its fragrance on their own faces. All is chaos until the baptismal party manages to reach the towering ambo that stands in the middle of the pewless hall. The bishop ascends its lower front steps, turns to face the whiteclad neophytes grouped at the bottom with their burning lamps and the boisterous faithful now held back by a phalanx of well-built acolytes and doorkeepers. Euphemius's mother has fainted and has been carried outside for air.

The bishop opens his arms to the neophytes and once again all burst into "Christ is risen," *Christos aneste*. He then affirms and seals their baptism after prayer, for all the faithful to see, with an authoritative gesture of paternity—laying his hand on each head, signing each oily forehead once again in the form of a cross, while booming out: "The servant of God is sealed with the Holy Spirit." To which all reply in a thunderous "Amen," and for the first time, the former catechumens receive and give the kiss of peace. Everyone is in tears.

While this continues, bread and wine are laid out on the holy table; the bishop then prays at great length over them after things quiet down, and the neophytes lead all to communion with Euphemius out in front. While his grandfather holds his lamp, Euphemius dines on the precious Body, whose true and undoubted member he has become; drinks the precious Blood of him in whom he himself now has died; and just this once drinks from another special cup— one containing milk and honey mixed as a gustatory icon of the promised land into which he and his colleagues finally have entered out of the desert through Jordan's waters. Then his mother (now recovered and somewhat pale, still insisting she had only stumbled) takes him home and puts him, fragrantly, to bed.

Euphemius has come a long way. He has passed from death into a life he lives still.

Appendix: Part Two
Bulletin Announcements

The following paragraphs are part of Three Days to Save, *a pamphlet about the Triduum (published by LTP). It is intended for distribution to parishioners on Palm Sunday as an invitation to keep the Triduum in their lives and to join the assembly for the various liturgies. These excerpts are given to assist parishes that might want to create their own invitations for the parish bulletin; they may not be reproduced in this form, however, without permission.*

What We Do from Holy Thursday to Easter Sunday

Holy Thursday brings the end to Lent. That night we begin the Three Days that are the center of our year. Why are these Three Days so important? What do they mean for you? You are invited to make these Three Days different from all the days of the year.

Adults in the community are invited to plan ahead so that the whole time from Thursday night until the Easter Vigil is free of social engagements, free even of work, free of entertainment, free of meals except for the simplest nourishment. We are asked to fast during Good Friday and to continue fasting, if possible, all through Holy Saturday as strictly as we can, so that we come hungry and full of excitement to the Easter Vigil. We make Good Friday and Holy Saturday free for prayer and reflection and preparation and silence. The church is getting ready.

Whether you are young or old, currently active in the parish or not, please set these days aside. All of us should know that our presence for the liturgies is not just by invitation. We are all needed here. All of us need this whole community together on its greatest days.

On these Three Days, we gather a number of times. Together we hear some of the church's most beautiful prayers and scriptures and we make some of our finest music. Please look closely at the parish schedule and make plans to take part in the various liturgies and other gatherings of Holy Thursday night, Good Friday and Holy Saturday. Above all, come on Saturday night for the Vigil.

We Begin as Holy Thursday Ends

Thursday evening we enter into this Triduum together. After listening to the scriptures, we do something strange: We wash feet. Some of us go down on our knees with pitchers of water, basins and towels. Jesus gave us this image of what the church is supposed to look like, feel like, act like. This is rehearsal for Christian life, as is the next thing we do, a collection for the poor.

Later we celebrate the eucharist. The evening liturgy has no ending: Whether we stay to pray awhile or leave, we are now in the quiet and peace and glory of the Triduum.

And We Continue through Good Friday and Holy Saturday

We gather quietly on Friday and listen to scripture. We pray at length for all the world's needs. Then there is another once-a-year event: The holy cross is held up in our midst and we come forward one by one to do reverence with a kiss or a bow or a genuflection.

We continue in fasting and prayer and vigil, in rest and quiet through Saturday. This Saturday for us is like God's rest at the end of creation. It is Christ's repose in the tomb.

Until the Night between Saturday and Sunday

Hungry now and excited, the church gathers in the darkness and lights a new fire and a great candle that will make this night bright for us. We listen to some of the most powerful scriptures in the Bible, then we pray to all our saints to stand with us as we go to the font and bless the waters. There the catechumens are baptized and anointed. These are the moments when death and life meet, when we reject evil and give our promises to God. Together we go to the table and celebrate the Easter eucharist. Easter Sunday begins and we are ready for Fifty Days of rejoicing.

Appendix: Part Three
Homily for Palm Sunday

This text is reproduced with permission from The Liturgical Conference; it appeared in the March 1991 edition of Homily Service.

Today is the sixth and the last of the Sundays of Lent. We know it also by other names. It is called Palm Sunday because the first thing that we do when we gather this day is to take up palms and tell the story of how Jesus once came into the holy city, Jerusalem, riding over a carpet of branches, cheered by people waving branches.

Today also is known as Passion Sunday because the gospel story read today is always the long account of Jesus' passion as told by Matthew, by Mark or by Luke.

Today knows other events. This is the last Sunday when we will dismiss those catechumens who, at the start of this Lent, were chosen or "elected" for baptism at Easter. Next Sunday and from then on they will not be dismissed after the homily but will stay with us and do all that baptized people do. They will begin to keep each Sunday by joining the church to give God thanks and praise at this table, over bread and wine, which we eat and drink and so become, little by little, ourselves the body of Christ.

Today marks the beginning of the days we call Holy Week. That name, Holy Week, can be misleading or it can be a rich insight into these days. It can mislead if we think of the time from today until next Sunday, Easter Sunday, as one segment of time that day by day tries to tell the story of the passion, death and resurrection of Jesus. That's not really what happens here. Rather, we have a week that splits in two on Thursday night and each one of us ought to know how and why. That will tell us what puts the "holy" in Holy Week.

Until Thursday night it is Lent. The Forty Days right now are down to their last five days. Thursday evening Lent ends. If we have kept these days so far with various kinds of fasting, various forms of almsgiving, and times of prayer each day, then we are near the end and can perhaps put on an extra burst of energy and so finish this great lenten contest smiling and exuberant to have done penance and turned the world a bit upside-down.

And if we have not kept these days so well, or perhaps not at all, if we have forgotten to pray, neglected to fast, not gotten around to all the ways alms can be given, then the news is good: Five days, counting today, to go! It isn't too late at all. Time enough remains to discover what hunger feels like—bodily hunger and other hungers too. Time remains for that spring-cleaning of house and wallet and life that Lent makes almost appealing to us who are too heavily laden with possessions and near-addictions. Time remains also for quiet, for taking out the Bible and reading these passion accounts, reading here and there in Paul, reading psalms and prophets, and quietly reflecting on these words and stories and letting them help us to pray. Time remains. Five days of Lent to conclude your Forty Days, or Five Days to be your Forty Days.

But that brings us only to Thursday evening. That is the reason we say that this so-called Holy Week is really two very different pieces of time. For when Lent ends, we move without stopping for breath into the three days that are for us the heart and soul of the entire year. The church calls them a "triduum," just the Latin for "three days." But it calls them also an "Easter Triduum" or a "Paschal Triduum." What that means is that they are about the paschal mystery, the passover mystery, the way life and death and resurrection, our own, our church's, our human race's, get all tangled up in the life and death and resurrection of the one who is truly God and truly human, Jesus.

On Thursday night we walk out of Lent into these three holiest days, walk into them singing: "We should glory in the cross of our Lord Jesus Christ." And there it is, in one part of one sentence from Paul: Our glory is in the cross. The cross is our glory. Somehow that is what it comes to for us, the transforming cross that never ceases to be the cross, the death that is death itself, all the ways death reigns in this poor world, but we look at it and we say, "Glory".

From Thursday night until Sunday afternoon, it is this Triduum. We will gather here Thursday night and Friday afternoon and then in the darkness of Saturday night. These are liturgies we do not celebrate three or four times each day so that it is convenient for us to come. We do it once and we hope that all of us can be together, most especially at the Easter Vigil. That gathering of the church between Saturday evening and Sunday morning is the life that nourishes our whole year, all our days. It is when we come to spend some good time in the reading of scripture, and then go finally to the baptismal font where our catechumens are challenged to renounce evil, to believe in Father and Son and Spirit, and so to die in the waters and live forever in Christ. We do the liturgies of these days only once because who would have the energy to do them again? We do them once because we wish that this whole parish be, this once in the year, all together here to do scripture and baptism and eucharist.

And we dare to do these liturgies just once and to say that we should all be here because of something that we so easily overlook. It is: What else could we possibly find to do? That is the key to getting from the end of Lent back into life in this world. We have to know that life-as-usual stops from Thursday evening to Easter Sunday. Or perhaps it doesn't stop, but we do. We drop out. We do not do on this Good Friday and this Holy Saturday what we do on any other Friday and Saturday of the year. So we are not ever trying to work in "going to church" among a hundred other things. No. The decks are clear. Lots of things in our lives have been closed down. We are free.

We have to know this: The way these three days are kept is not only with the liturgies here in this assembly. For these to have any sense at all to them, the three days have to be kept in our lives. A generation ago, at Vatican II, the world's bishops had a great and ancient insight into this. They said these strange words: "Let the paschal fast be kept sacred. Let it be celebrated everywhere on Good Friday and, where possible, prolonged throughout Holy Saturday." They spoke not of a lenten fast but of a paschal fast, an Easter fast. What's that? And they spoke not just of fasting, but of "celebrating" this particular fast. What sort of fasting is celebrated? It is the fasting of excitement and expectation, of butterflies in the stomach because of what is about to happen. It is fasting from food, yes, but fasting also from work, and from entertainment and distraction. It is getting real hungry. It is clearing the mind and the heart. It is being famished for the word of God.

So the invitation to us Christians is to leave all we can of the normal on Thursday night. Off and on through those next three days, we'll meet here. You have your schedules of liturgies and other times of prayer. But it is the times between the liturgies that make the liturgies possible. Let all of us together find again and anew what is this glory that is ours in the cross of our Lord Jesus Christ.

Appendix: Part Four
Resources for Parish and Home Use

For Background on the Triduum

Adolf Adam. *The Liturgical Year: Its History and Its Meaning after the Reform of the Liturgy.* Collegeville: Pueblo Publishing, 1981. A fine general introduction.

God's Mercy Endures Forever: Guidelines on the Presentation of Jews and Judaism in Catholic Preaching. Washington DC: United States Catholic Conference, 1988. Important for both the approach and for specifics regarding the passion narrative.

Aidan Kavanagh. *The Shape of Baptism: The Rite of Christian Initiation.* Collegeville: Pueblo Publishing, 1978. Theology from the liturgy, the finest foundation available for understanding the reform expressed in the RCIA.

Henry Ansgar Kelly. *The Devil at Baptism.* Ithaca: Cornell University Press, 1985. Scholarly study of the language and meaning of the exorcisms and renunciations.

Adrian Nocent. *The Liturgical Year.* Collegeville: The Liturgical Press, 1977. Rich resource of history and theology in four volumes; volume 3 contains notes on the Triduum.

John T. Pawlikowski and James A. Wilde. *When Catholics Speak about Jews.* Chicago: LTP, 1987. Practical approach to what we say about Judaism in prayer and preaching throughout the year with specific attention to Lent and the Triduum.

Alexander Schmemann. *Great Lent: Journey to Pascha.* Crestwood NY: St. Vladimir's Seminary Press, 1974. This is from the Orthodox perspective but is filled with insight for Western understanding.

Alexander Schmemann. *Of Water and the Spirit.* Crestwood NY: St. Vladimir's Seminary Press, 1974. The meaning of baptism in the Orthodox church as manifest in the liturgy itself.

Kenneth Stevenson. *Jerusalem Revisited: The Liturgical Meaning of Holy Week.* Washington DC: The Pastoral Press, 1988. Strong in its insight into the history of the rites.

Thomas Talley. *The Origins of the Liturgical Year.* Collegeville: Pueblo Publishing, 1986. Excellent presentation of current scholarship, including the evolution of the paschal season.

For Preparing the Triduum
Rupert Berger and Hans Hollerweger, eds. *Celebrating the Easter Vigil.* Collegeville: Pueblo Publishing, 1983. Uneven, but worthwhile as a reference.

Congregation for Divine Worship. *Paschalis sollemnitas, Circular Letter Concerning the Preparation and Celebration of the Easter Triduum.* Washington DC: United States Catholic Conference, 1988. This document ranks rather low on the scale of official documents, but serves to consolidate much that had appeared previously.

Gabe Huck and Mary Ann Simcoe, eds. *A Triduum Sourcebook.* Chicago: LTP, 1983. (Also available: *A Lent Sourcebook* [two volumes] and *An Easter Sourcebook.*) These are like an Office of Readings for each season, containing prose and poetry from scripture and every period of the tradition.

Don A. Neumann. *Holy Week in the Parish.* Collegeville: The Liturgical Press, 1991. The story of how one parish, with much effort and enthusiasm, keeps the Triduum.

Sourcebook for Sundays and Seasons. Chicago: LTP. An annual book to assist in the preparation of the liturgies.

For the Home
Catholic Household Blessings and Prayers. Washington DC: United States Catholic Conference, 1988. (Available from LTP.) The home ritual for Catholics in the United States: daily, seasonal, festival and occasional rites and prayers, including several for the paschal season.

Gabe Huck. *An Introduction to Lent and Eastertime.* Chicago: LTP, 1987. A pamphlet for parishioners introducing Lent, Triduum and Eastertime.

Gabe Huck and Mary Ann Simcoe, eds. *A Triduum Sourcebook.* Noted above.

Keeping Lent, Triduum and Eastertime. Chicago: LTP, 1988. A small prayer book for daily use during these seasons. Available in English or Spanish.

Three Days to Save. Chicago: LTP, 1992. A Palm Sunday handout that explains the Triduum and urgently invites all to be part of it both at home and at the church.

Appendix: Part Five
Priority Chart

This chart provides a quick and necessarily general look at the various times when large or small assemblies may take place during the Triduum. It has been adapted from the 1991 *Sourcebook for Sundays and Seasons* (LTP).

	Primary events	Second events that are excellent additions in every parish	Further possibilities for parishes that already have the other elements
Holy Thursday	Evening Mass of the Lord's Supper	Night prayer	Eucharistic Adoration
Good Friday	Celebration of the Lord's Passion	Morning Prayer Night Prayer	Office of Readings Midday Prayer
Holy Saturday	Easter Vigil	Morning Prayer Preparation Rites for the Elect	Office of Readings Midday Prayer Evening Prayer
Easter Sunday	Mass(es) of Easter Evening Prayer (Baptismal Vespers)	Morning Prayer	Blessing of Easter Foods Midday Prayer

Appendix: Part Six
A Sample Triduum Schedule

Parishioners should receive, well in advance, an attractive and understandable schedule for the Triduum. Principal events should stand out and brief words of explanation can be included. The whole tone, in appearance as in words, should be one of urgent invitation. The following example is adapted from the 1989 *Sourcebook for Sundays and Seasons.*

Holy Thursday, Date

6:00 PM Parish Meal

We conclude Lent by joining together in the cafeteria to share a final meal before entering into the paschal fast.

8:00 PM Mass of the Lord's Supper

    Welcoming the Easter Triduum
    Liturgy of the word
    Washing of feet
    Collection for the poor
    Liturgy of the eucharist
    Vigiling and the paschal fast begin

The church will remain open throughout the night as we begin to keep watch in prayer and fasting in the spirit of Gethsemane. Adoration of the Blessed Sacrament ends at 11:00 PM.

11:00 PM Night Prayer

Good Friday, Date

The church will remain open throughout the day as we continue to keep watch in prayer and fasting.

9:00 AM Morning Prayer

12:00 Noon Midday Prayer

3:00 PM The Celebration of the Passion of the Lord

    Prostration in silence
    Liturgy of the word
    Intercession for the world
    Veneration of the cross
    Communion
    Vigiling and fasting continue

5:00 PM Parish Meal

All are invited to join together in the school cafeteria to share a simple meal in the spirit of the paschal fast.

8:00 PM Night Prayer
The church will remain open throughout the night as we continue to keep watch in fasting and prayer.

Holy Saturday, Date

The church will remain open throughout the day as we continue to keep watch in fasting and prayer.

9:00 AM Morning Prayer

12:00 Noon Midday Prayer

3:00 PM The Rites of Preparation of the Elect

We gather as a parish with the elect for a final time before their baptism, confirmation and eucharist tonight.

5:00 PM **Parish Meal**

All are invited to join together in the school cafeteria to share a simple meal in the spirit of the paschal fast.

Nightwatch of the Resurrection, Date

10:00 PM The Easter Vigil

> Vigiling continues in the darkness
> Easter bonfire
> Giving thanks for the light
> Proclamation of scripture
> Blessing the water
> Liturgy of baptism and confirmation
> Liturgy of the eucharist

A reminder: Please bring a glass vigil light or other container to bring home the Easter fire. Easter water in containers will be provided. Also please remember to bring your Easter foods for the blessing of foods tonight.

Following the liturgy: Parish Meal

The eucharist breaks our fast. The feast begins. All are invited to join together in the school cafeteria and to share in the Easter breakfast. Bring treats! Our guests of honor this night are the newly baptized.

Easter Sunday, Date

8:00 AM **Morning Prayer**

10:00 AM **Easter Mass**

12:00 Noon **Easter Mass**

A reminder: the blessing of Easter foods and baskets will take place after every Mass.

The church will remain open throughout the day. You are invited to come visit with family and guests.

6:00 PM **Evening Prayer and Easter Caroling**

Appendix: Part Seven
Recipe for Eucharistic Bread

Preheat oven to 400°.

In a bowl, mix ⅔ cup of white flour and ⅓ cup of wheat flour (it helps if flour is ice cold).

In a cold bowl, mix the flour mixture and ½ to ⅔ cup of sparkling water. (Use only ½ cup of water and then add a little more if mixture is too dry.) Be sure that the water is also very cold.

This should form a ball but not be wet.

Spray a 9-inch pie pan with Pam, wipe out and then flatten ball into pie plate.

Score the dough into 100 pieces.

Bake for 10 minutes; prick with a fork in many places, then flip over in pan. Bake for another 5 minutes; flip right side up. Bake another 15 minutes for a total of 30 minutes.

Let cool and wrap in wax paper, then in foil if bread is to be frozen.

Prepared by Robert Piercy

Appendix: Part Eight
Easter Candle Directions

This plan for the making of a parish Easter candle is taken from the January/February 1981 issue of Liturgy 80. *The author/candle-maker is Rev. Jonathan Scalone,* TOR.

Making a majestic paschal candle is not very different from making a smaller candle. You will simply be dealing with larger quantities or larger sizes of materials. The cost is about $80 (depending on current prices) and most of the material can be recycled. I suggest that if you accept the challenge to make this candle you use the resource people of your community who have skills in the area of candlemaking. Even if you never have made a candle before, it is possible to make such a large candle; I would recommend a basic candle-making book, purchased at a local craft store, as a resource for this project.

Materials Needed:

All amounts and exact measures will vary with the size and width of your candle mold (the sewer pipe).

One polyurethane (hard plastic) sewer pipe to be used for the mold. It comes in four-inch and six-inch diameters. Length varies. I suggest beginning with an eight-foot length. This can be purchased at plumbing supply stores.

Wick. Leaded wick, approximately four times longer than the actual length of the candle you want. You will need to purchase a number of strands of wicking because it must be braided with three or four strands per braid. I recommend the four-strand braiding. You may find a roll of wicking with yards of wick on it, but wicking often comes in small packages of predetermined lengths. If that is your situation, make a few braided wicks, then tie them tightly together to form one long wick about a foot longer than what you actually need to pass through the mold.

A roll of masking tape.

Modeling clay, about five or six pounds. (Do not use "play dough" or the homemade variety.)

Two strong wooden sticks, longer than the diameter of your pipe.

Paraffin wax, approximately one-half pound of wax per inch of candle at a six-inch diameter (plus about three-quarters of a pound extra to allow for filling in the air pocket). This is sold in craft stores and usually comes in large slabs. Notice the color of the slab for that is the shade of white that the candle actually will be unless you decide to color your wax.

Wax hardener, "styrene" (check instructions on package for needed amounts).

Scissors, knife, saw (to cut the pipe).

Candy or wax thermometer.

Metal or plastic wash bucket.

Two bags of ice.

Large container(s) to melt wax. All wax must be melted at the same time at a 125-degree temperature for the first pouring.

Something to stir the wax with while it melts.

At least two one-quart pitchers or old coffeepots, preferably metal.

Acrylic paints for the decorating of the candle.

Two people on the actual day of melting and pouring.

Work space in a room in which the candle won't be disturbed for at least a week while the wax is hardening. The room should be cool to facilitate the hardening of the wax. Check ceiling height in relation to the desired height of your candle.

Wax coloring if you decide to color your candle. A white coloring is available that makes the candle more opaque though I have found the natural whiteness of the paraffin ideal. Wax scent and wax gloss are other optional equipment.

The Stand

The principle to keep in mind is that you need enough weight in the base to counterbalance the final weight of your candle. And the stand must hold the candle securely in place. I suggest having coasters or small ballbearing wheels on the bottom of your stand. I have used wooden logs cut at various lengths: the shortest approximately one foot, the tallest approximately 18 inches. These are affixed to a base. It is an inexpensive stand and easy to make. See diagram A.

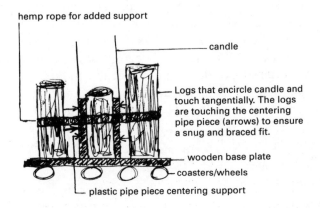

hemp rope for added support

candle

A.

Logs that encircle candle and touch tangentially. The logs are touching the centering pipe piece (arrows) to ensure a snug and braced fit.

wooden base plate

coasters/wheels

plastic pipe piece centering support

The Candle Making

The process that will be described may seem overwhelming at first. It isn't. It takes about five hours from start to finish, presuming you have all your materials on hand.

1. Decide on the height of the candle you want, taking into consideration the height of your church ceiling, the height of your stand and the liturgical space available.

2. Considering the height you want your candle to be, cut one foot of the plastic pipe and save it for a centering support for your base. (If you want an eight-foot candle and your pipe is eight feet tall, you will have to buy some extra pipe to be used in the base.) In the base itself, this one-foot pipe piece allows for a snug, secure fit and added support.

3. Wash the inside of the actual mold piece of pipe by passing well-soaked soapy rags through it. Rinse the inside of the mold with fresh water and dry it completely.

4. Break your slabs of paraffin into more manageable pieces and begin melting the wax in your melting container. I don't recommend using beeswax from leftover candle stubs because it is much softer. Regarding melting procedures, a double boiler is recommended, but if you have sufficient experience with melting wax, you can use a direct, low flame. Use your candy or wax thermometer to keep track of the wax temperature (125 degrees is the temperature you want before pouring it into the candle mold). *Caution: Do not exceed this temperature.* Stir the melting wax occasionally. (The melting process takes about two hours.)

5. Braid the wick using three single strands or, preferably, four single strands to form one thick braided wick. Make it one foot longer than the mold itself.

6. Work/knead all of your clay together and make a large pancake 1½ inches thick and six inches larger than the circumference of your plastic sewer-pipe mold.

7. Tie and knot about four inches of your braided wick to one of the sticks, at the stick's center. Working from the uncut end of the pipe, pass the wick through the entire length of the pipe. Center the stick on the diameter of the pipe and tape it securely to the sides of the pipe. Make sure that the wick is in the exact center of the mold. Repeat at the other end of the mold and at this end pull the wick taut before tying it to the stick and taping the stick to the side of the mold. The wick now is centered to ensure proper burning when the candle is lit.

8. The uncut end of your pipe is the top of your candle, the end you actually will light. Take your clay pancake, center it to the wick at this top of your candle and pack the clay firmly

over the side of the pipe and stick. Pack this as tightly as possible to the sides of the mold, coming up on the sides of the mold about three inches. Pay special attention to the place where the clay, stick and mold meet. This clay-ended top is the seal that holds the wax in the mold. What you now have before you looks like diagram B.

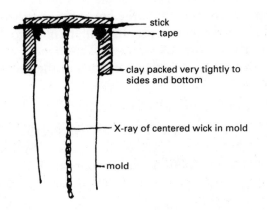

stick
tape
clay packed very tightly to sides and bottom
X-ray of centered wick in mold
mold

B.

9. Place the clay-ended top in a bucket, and secure the mold vertically to the wall by taping it so it won't move. Make sure it is secured to the wall as firmly as possible. I use a corner of the room for this anchoring procedure. See diagram C.

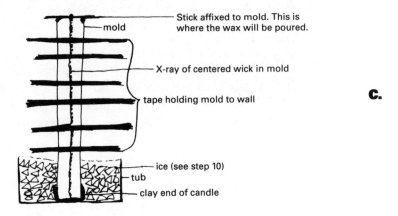

mold
Stick affixed to mold. This is where the wax will be poured.
X-ray of centered wick in mold
tape holding mold to wall
ice (see step 10)
tub
clay end of candle

C.

10. When all the wax is melted to 125 degrees, get ready to pour. Add the wax hardener and let it melt in the melted wax. Stirring will facilitate this. (It is not necessary to add a scent, but if one wishes to do so, add this to the melted wax at the last possible minute, making sure that it, too, dissolves in the melted wax.) Add the bags of ice to the bucket with the mold to cool the lower section of the mold. See diagram C.

11. As smoothly as you can, transfer the wax from the melting-containers to the mold with the help of the pitchers. Pour the wax in slowly and consistently. Fill the mold to the very brim and let it stand. (A water-bucket-brigade procedure will help here: One fills the pitchers and the other pours the wax.)

12. Leave the candle alone and let it harden.

13. You should have extra wax left over. During the course of the week, check your candle each day. An air pocket will form from the open pouring end of your candle downward.

    Sometimes you may have to poke through an initial layer of wax to find the air pocket. Repeat this procedure as needed during the week allowing 24 hours between these air-pocket fillings. About four pourings should do it.

14. After you have filled the candle for the last time, let it stand for an additional day or two. You will know the candle is ready to be removed from the mold by tapping the pipe. You will hear a crisp, sharp, somewhat hollow sound that indicates the wax has contracted away from the walls of the mold. Or simply wait for three or four days to ensure proper hardening.

15. Keep your candle vertical as much as possible when moving it. Unfasten it from the wall, all the while holding the mold. (If you have to move it horizontally, put a support board under it. See diagram D.) When the candle is lifted from the bucket, it will be quite heavy and cumbersome. You will

need a few strong people for this part. Invert your candle so that the clay (top end) now is pointing toward the ceiling. This is the top of your candle. While inverting it, give as much support to the center of the candle as possible. Now remove the clay, untape the sticks from the top and bottom of the mold, and be careful not to cut the wick at the top of the candle.

candle and mold

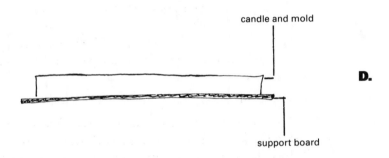

D.

support board

16. Try to be in a place where the mold can be lifted vertically from the candle. You'll need a ceiling clearance twice the height of your candle. If you attempt to remove the mold horizontally, take care to support the exposed candle as much as possible. Sometimes when removing the mold, the friction of the mold against the candle causes the mold to stick because some wax has melted. Just add some vegetable oil in the mold and slide the mold up and down until the oil lubricates the wax and enables you to lift the mold from the candle. Once the mold is off, wipe off the vegetable oil.

17. Mount your candle in your stand and give it the finishing touches. Completely clean and level the top of your candle. Trim the wick down to about one and one-half inches. Paint your design.

Care of Your Candle

1. Occasionally, trim the excess hard wax wall from the top of the candle. See diagram E. This wax wall results from the intermittent lighting of the candle at daily Masses.

E.

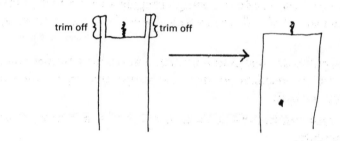

2. Burn the candle as constantly as possible at the Sunday Masses during Eastertime. Try not to extinguish it after each Mass. This will result in a more even burning of the wax.

3. Keep the candle away from direct sunlight and heating units. If the church is extremely hot during the summer, the candle may have to be moved to a cooler place temporarily. If your candle bows as a result of the summer heat, simply remove the candle from the stand and lay it on its side so that the bowed side is off the floor. Add supports as needed to hold the candle in place. The heat that bowed it will unbow it and make it flat again as it reacts with the weight of the candle. See diagram F. Unbowing will take a few days.

F.

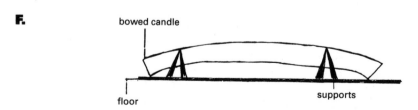

Appendix: Part Nine
Baptismal Garment Directions

This pattern for a baptismal garment is the work of Judy Dioszegi. It assumes that the work will be undertaken by an experienced person.

This pattern is designed to be enveloping. Sleeves should be full and the garment should be long—to the lower calf or ankle.

Make a paper pattern first (perhaps using brown wrapping paper). Adjustments and size differences can be worked out on this paper pattern.

This design fits an average to large person comfortably. For smaller people, reduce neckline ½-inch and proportion hem and sleeve length accordingly.

One garment requires three yards of 60-inch wide linen/polyester blend in white.

Instructions

Cut pattern according to diagram.

Fold fabric in half as indicated.

Smooth fabric and pin together sides.

Place paper pattern on fabric and pin in position.

It may be easier to sew top shoulder seam first and then cut away.

Finish all raw edges.

Seam at ⅝-inch.

If a larger neck opening is required, enlarge front opening by ½-inch as indicated by dotted line.

Finish neckline with a narrow hem or a simple binding applied to the inside turned edge.

Sew lower edge of sleeves. Bar tack or straight stitch at corner of sleeve and side seam for reinforcement. Clip corner to ease the fit. Turn sides back ½-inch and stitch at ¼-inch.

Make necessary adjustments for sleeve and hem length. Turn both back 1-inch and stitch at ¾-inch. Press well.

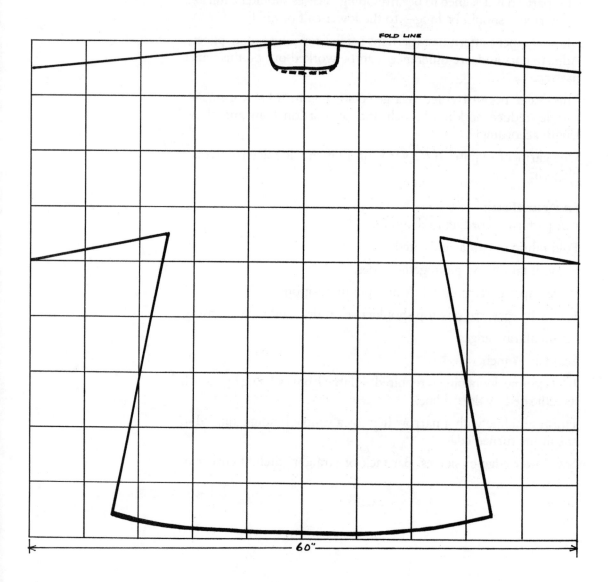

FOLD LINE

60"

First Reading   Genesis 1:1—2:2

Let us pray.

Like a mighty wind over waters
your spirit rushed about the chaos,
God of darkness and of light.
Day by day you labored
and day by day you found your work good.
Then on the sixth day you made the holy parents of us all,
Adam and Eve,
who on this night rejoiced
—as we in this church rejoice—
to see the gates of death broken down
and all the power of evil trampled
by our Lord Jesus Christ,
who lives and reigns with you, one God,
for ever and ever.

Second Reading   Genesis 22:1–18

Let us pray.

God of our ancestors:
What does it mean that you so put a parent to the test,
to command Abraham to take the child's life, even for you?
Are you not also a parent?
In this night's darkness
we want to know your beloved child Jesus,
who was bound Isaac-like to the wood of the cross
and so became the first-born of the dead,
first-born of those, countless as the stars,

among whom we would be counted.
Hear us, answer us,
for you are Lord for ever and ever.

Third Reading   Exodus 14:15—15:1

Let us pray.

This is the night, God of Israel,
when first you saved our ancestors,
when the throng of Jacob's descendants,
leaving slavery behind,
saw the mighty waters of the sea turn back
so they could pass.
We who keep vigil here tonight
have met death in the waters of baptism,
and there we have put on life itself,
your child Jesus.
With Jesus let us sing your praise
for ever and ever.

Fourth Reading   Isaiah 54:5–14

Let us pray.

In the secret and the darkness of this night,
you, our God, have embraced us,
thrown aside the whole past to love your world for ever.
This is the wedding night of the church,
and this great hall is our bridal chamber.
Pledge yourself to us
and to those who will tonight be baptized.
Pledge a love that will lead us in ways of justice,
in the very way of our Lord Jesus Christ

who lives and reigns with you, one God,
for ever and ever.

Fifth Reading   Isaiah 55:1–11

Let us pray.

God of mercy,
on this one night in all the year
we come together hungry and thirsty.
Over and over again we open the book of scripture
to devour your word,
to quench our thirst with your word.
Then let your words be on our lips
when we rise up and when we lie down,
when we are in our homes
and when we go on our way.
Then we shall proclaim that you are Lord
for ever and ever.

Sixth Reading   Baruch 3:9–15, 32—4:4

Let us pray.

In this night between death and life
we cling to you alone, God, wisdom,
mother to us all and light to our path.
Teach us the way of peace
that in households and among peoples
we may do what is pleasing to you.
We ask this through Christ our Lord.

Seventh Reading   Ezekiel 36:16–28

Let us pray.

With all our hearts, even our hearts of stone,
we ask you, Lord, that we might come this night
to the long-promised land, the land of milk and honey,
the land where your name is made holy in deeds of justice,
the hungry fed and the naked clothed,
prisoners set free, creation reverenced,
and all to share and share alike at your table.
This we ask, this we seek
through Christ our Lord.

Appendix: Part Eleven
Sacristan Notes

These notes are taken from the 1992 Sourcebook for Sundays and Seasons *by G. Thomas Ryan.*

The sacramentary and other official liturgical documentation should guide sacristans through these days.

Thursday evening (before Mass): "The tabernacle should be entirely empty." That implies that the veil is removed, the vigil light is removed, the doors are left open. That rubric, as well as the norms of the sacramentary for Lent, imply that the entire church is stripped and cleaned—without candles or cloths or any unnecessary furniture. This is not "iconoclasm" born of a distaste for sacred images, for we Catholics are not given to Puritanism. It is, rather, a bareness brought about by the discipline of giving undivided attention to the ritual actions and giving rise to a hunger for splendor, a longing for things to be whole again.

Thursday evening (for the end of Mass): The place for the transfer of the eucharist is described as "a chapel suitably decorated" and "conducive to prayer and meditation" (*Circular Letter,* #49). What is "suitably decorated"? Candles always are appropriate; they seem to beckon us to the eschaton. Save the lilies for Saturday night.

Thursday evening (after Mass): Crosses are to be removed from the church or veiled. It also is customary to remove holy water from the fonts to await the Easter water. The removal of water or crosses, however, is a logical part of the church cleaning earlier in Lent or before Ash Wednesday. There should be little to strip from the church tonight except the altar cloth and the furniture used in the washing of the feet. Anything not part of the building itself (credence tables, kneelers, etc.) should be removed. The few items needed for the celebration tomorrow can be brought in for the service and then taken away. Although there is no ceremony for removing the altar cloth, strip the altar with great reverence and dignity. This simple action was for years a sign of our entering into the paschal fast. It took place while singing Psalm 22. The psalm still may be prayed by those performing this ministry.

Thursday midnight: In the chapel where the reserved sacrament is kept, all candles, except for the candle near the tabernacle, are extinguished at the conclusion of eucharistic adoration or night prayer (whichever comes later). All other decorations are taken from the eucharistic chapel before the first hour of prayer on Friday.

Friday (before the Celebration of the Lord's Passion): Only those items of furniture needed for the rite are set out. Candles are to be ready near the cross for its solemn entrance, and an altar cloth is kept to the side for later use. All else is bare.

Friday (for communion rite): At the conclusion of the rite, any remaining eucharist is brought to a separate, private place to be kept for viaticum. This must not be the eucharistic chapel, for the reservation is not provided to allow for visitation or private prayer.

Friday (after the Celebration): Everything is completely stripped except for a shrine of the holy cross. The cross (which was carried in during the celebration) is to be (with lighted candles and perhaps burning incense) in a place conducive both to quiet prayer and to reverencing the cross with a touch or kiss. The *Circular Letter* (#71) suggests that the cross be placed in the now-empty eucharistic chapel. If the cross is a stationary one—for example, the one suspended over the altar—then candles now grace it.

Saturday in general: The church should be decorated as late as possible so that it is bare for most of the liturgy of the hours, preparatory rites or any other assembly. The enshrined cross remains in its place of honor with or without lighted candles.

Saturday morning: The *Circular Letter* (#74) suggests that an image or two may be introduced into the space for the whole day:

> The image of Christ crucified or lying in the tomb, or the descent into hell, which mystery Holy Saturday recalls, as also an image of the sorrowful Virgin Mary, can be placed in the church for the veneration of the faithful.

Saturday night (Vigil): The *Ceremonial of Bishops* (#48) contains an interesting note reminding many old-time sacristans of hectic Vigils long ago: The rubrics ban the use of flowers from "Ash Wednesday until the Gloria at the Easter Vigil." For centuries, a reverent procession of flower bearers and veil removers (recall the rubrics regarding the removal of veils from the statues) took place at the Gloria. The possibility for this activity still exists.

Rites Form Architecture

Good ritual celebrations demand appropriate spaces, and the liturgies of the Triduum point the way in several important areas. This is not the time of the year for pastors and liturgical planners to worry about renovation plans, but it is the perfect time to jot down notes about what would have enhanced and facilitated the prayer of the assembly.

Thursday: The place of reposition is the eucharistic chapel if this is separate from the main worship space. A parish that uses a side altar for the tabernacle faces a difficult challenge at times like this. It probably should set up another room for reservation. And then it should add this to the list of renovation topics. The liturgy of the church does not countenance the reservation of the eucharist in the same room in which it is celebrated.

Friday: The size and location of the cross that will grace the worship space is related directly to the veneration on this day. A suspended cross must be attached in such a way that the assembly can touch or kiss it—no substitute cross should be brought in for this moment. The Roman Rite's preference for the church's regular cross to be a processional cross—not a permanently fixed cross—rises in part from this rite and its centrality in linking the parish to its cross.

Saturday night (and other days): Because every household should come to the Vigil, a child-care facility will be needed. This is not peripheral to good liturgy. For 20 years, the *Rite of Baptism for Children* (#14) has called for an auxiliary room where children and infants should be taken until the time of baptism. The possible presence of infants to be baptized at the Vigil lends further strength to this Triduum exigency. (Of course, restroom facilities should be nearby.)

Saturday night (Fire): The fire and the lighting and praise of the Easter candle make particular architectural and landscaping demands. Renovation plans must consider the full observance of this liturgy, with all gathered in a place separate from the main space.

Saturday night (Water): An immersion font is called for. The National Statutes for the Catechumenate, approved by the United States Conference of Bishops in 1986, tell us that immersion is the preferred mode of baptism (statute #17). Baptism by immersion—our worldwide ancient tradition—is now a national priority. Immersion does not necessarily mean full submersion. The "immersion baptism" mosaics of many early baptistries show people standing in water, usually up to their knees, with water being poured over their heads, so that the water runs over their bodies as a "robe of glory." Committees continue to argue over the best place for the font, but it certainly is not right next to the other sacred furnishings. If you are constructing a font for this occasion, be aware that front and center is not always best. Allow this sacred action to unfold in its own area of the church, one that would allow for processions both to and from the site.